The Complete Guide To
RAISING PET BIRDS FOR PROFIT

The Greatest
Backyard Business Ever!

By James McDonald

Brentwood House Publishing
P.O. Box 291992
Kerrville, Texas 78028

Copyright © 2003 by James McDonald.

All rights reserved. No part of this book may be reproduced or transmitted in any form or by any means, electronic or mechanical, including photocopying, recording, or by any information storage or retrieval system without permission in writing from the publisher.

Library of Congress Control Number: 2003110675
ISBN 0-9743904-0-2

Published by: Brentwood House Publishing, P. O. Box 291992, Kerrville, Texas 78029

Although the author and publisher have made every effort to ensure the accuracy and completeness of information contained in this book, we assume no responsibility for errors, inaccuracies, omissions, or any inconsistency herein. Any slights of people, places, or organizations are unintentional.

Breeding birds is not a get rich scheme and should not be considered as such. It is a proven business that has a long history behind it. Your success can be determined to a large degree by the effort and devotion you put forth.

Printed in the United States of America

About The Author

James McDonald is a recognized authority with over 25 years of experience in the field of exotic birds and animals, having sold approximately one million birds during that time. Not only has he been successful in breeding many different species of exotic birds and animals, but he built a very profitable nationwide wholesale distributorship of pet birds. He has given lectures on breeding and raising exotic birds to veterinary classes at Texas A&M University and has spoken at numerous seminars and events throughout the country, including symposiums at such places as Purdue University. James has authored many articles on the subject of exotic birds and has been written about in newspapers and magazines, and he has appeared on television and news programs featuring the exotic bird business.

Having been raised on a farm, his love for animals came naturally. But that farm background also taught him that it was extremely difficult to make a profit with animals that were sold by the pound, because most of those animals consumed so much costly feed that by the time they reached a marketable size, there was very little profit to be made. Hence, he looked for something that was not a fad, that had a good history with a proven track record behind it, that had a strong demand and could be sold by the head and not by the pound. Exotic birds were the answer. They had a high profit margin and could be sold when they were young. Through the years he has willingly shared his extensive knowledge of exotic birds with others and has been instrumental in helping many people to build a profitable business with the various species of pet birds included in the following pages.

Dedication

This book is dedicated to my loving wife Brenda, whose role has been that of a wife, mom, secretary, salesman, janitor, grounds keeper, and everything else that goes with running your own bird business, as well as my best friend. She has been a jewel. Without her, my success would have been meaningless as well as impossible.

Acknowledgments

The reader would become board if I even began to name the scores of people that have contributed to my learning and educational process in the pet bird business, which in turn made this book possible. As a wholesale distributor of pet birds, I literally cannot remember all the fine people that I have bought birds from through the years. Many of the customers that we shipped birds to became not only great customers, but true and loyal friends as well. To those people I express my deepest thanks.

A special thanks also goes to Joyce Van Huss, Jonny Morris, Homer Heidle, Roger and Laurie Schoppe, June and Jimmy Vannoy, Ronald and Betty Tucker, as well as Leary and Sandra Sooter.

Contents

Part I

Introduction

Chapter 1
   Raising Exotic Birds for Profit 17
      Pet Industry Facts 21
      So Why Choose Birds? 22

Chapter 2
   Why Start With Parakeets, Cockatiels,
   Lovebirds Or Zebra Finches? 27

Chapter 3
   Can I Make A Profit Breeding Birds? 35
      Parakeets 36
      Cockatiels 38
      Lovebirds 40
      Zebra Finches 42

Chapter 4
   Different Ways
   In Which To Market Your Birds 47
      The Bird Buyer 47
      Selling Directly to Pet Shops 50
      Bird Marts, Pet Expos and Bird Fairs 51
      The Overlooked Markets 52
      Retail 53

Part II

Chapter 5
   Becoming A Wholesale Distributor
   Of Pet Birds 57

The greatest backyard business ever!

Chapter 6
How To Build Your Markets And
Your Customer Base 63
    Pet Bird Magazines 63
    Pet Trade Publications 66
    Trade Shows 68
    Business Lists 69

Chapter 7
Getting Started Buying Birds;
The Need For A Warehouse 77
    Grading and Sorting 87
    Shipping Your Birds 93
    Shipping Crates 94
    Shipping Requirements 99
    Shipping C.O.D vs. Open Account 100
    The Delivery Van or Truck 101

Part III

Chapter 8
Breeding Birds
Colony Breeding vs. Cage Breeding 105
    Advantages of cage breeding. 106
    Disadvantages of cage breeding 106
    Advantages of colony breeding 107
    Disadvantages of colony breeding 107
    Housing Requirements 111
    Climate Control and Ventilation 112
    Lighting Requirements 115
    Rodents 117
    Nutrition 118
    Labels on Feed Mixes 121
    Supplements To The Diet 125
    Acquiring Your Breeding Stock 128

Chapter 9
Breeding Parakeets 139
- Breeding Parakeets In Colonies 139
- Parakeet Nestboxes 140
- Feeding and Watering Parakeets 141
- Breeding Age Of Parakeets............................. 144
- Determining The Age Of Parakeets 144
- Sexing Parakeets 146
- Putting Your Parakeets To Work 146
- Working Your Nestboxes 148
- Resting Your Birds 151
- Cage Breeding Parakeets 152
- The Cage Breeding Unit 153
- Feeding 156
- Breeding Age Of Birds In Cages..................... 157
- Putting Your Birds To Work In Cages 157
- Working Your Nestboxes In Cage Breeding.... 158
- Resting Your Birds In Cage Breeding 160

Chapter 10
Breeding Cockatiels 161
- Breeding Cockatiels In Colonies 161
- Cockatiel Nestboxes 162
- Feeding and Watering Cockatiels 163
- Breeding Age Of Cockatiels 166
- Sexing Your Cockatiels 167
- Determining The Age Of Cockatiels................ 169
- Putting Your Cockatiels To Work 169
- Working Your Nestboxes 172
- Resting Your Birds 176
- Cage Breeding Cockatiels 178
- The Cage Breeding Unit 178
- Feeding 179
- Breeding Age Of Cockatiels In Cages 179
- Putting Your Birds To Work In Cages 180
- Working Your Nestboxes In Cage Breeding.... 180
- Resting Your Birds In Cage Breeding 181

The greatest backyard business ever!

Chapter 11
Breeding Lovebirds 183
Breeding Lovebirds In Colonies 183
Lovebird Nestboxes 184
Feeding And Watering Lovebirds 185
Breeding Age Of Lovebirds 188
Sexing Your Lovebirds 188
Determining The Age Of Lovebirds 190
Putting Your Lovebirds To Work 190
Working Your Nestboxes 192
Resting Your Lovebirds 194
Cage Breeding Lovebirds 195
The Cage Breeding Unit 196
Feeding 197
Breeding Age Of Lovebirds In Cages 197
Putting Your Birds To Work In Cages 197
Working Your Nestboxes In Cages 197
Resting Your Lovebirds In Cages 198

Chapter 12
Breeding Zebra Finches 199
Breeding Zebra Finches In Colonies 199
Zebra Finch Nestboxes 200
Feeding And Watering Zebra Finches 201
Breeding Age Of Zebra Finches 204
Sexing Zebra Finches 204
Determining The Age Of Zebra Finches 204
Putting Your Zebra Finches To Work 205
Working Your Nestboxes 208
Resting Your Birds 209
Cage Breeding Zebra Finches............................ 210

Chapter 13
Health Problems 213
- Characteristics Of A Sick Bird 213
- Common Problems You May Encounter 216
- Egg Binding 216
- Molting 217
- French Molt 218
- Diarrhea 218
- Overgrown or Deformed Beaks 219
- Overgrown Nails 219
- External Parasites 220
- Internal Parasites 220

Chapter 14
Managing And Upgrading Your Birds 223
- Our Responsibility 226

Chapter 15
Decision Time 229
- Not The Ending, But The Beginning 229

Appendix 233
- Testimonials 233
- Veterinary Medicine Diagnostic Labs 239
- Equipment and Supplies 249
- Quick Order Form 251

The greatest backyard business ever!

PART I

INTRODUCTION

This book was written as a practical guide for those interested in the breeding, raising and selling of exotic birds-mainly parakeets, cockatiels, finches and lovebirds for profit. It makes no difference if you are sixteen or seventy six, male or female, live in the city or country, if you enjoy the wonders of nature and have a sincere desire to be in business for yourself, this book was written specifically for you. It is not written in some far out technical jargon or academic terminology, but in an easy to understand style with plain and simple, down to earth language.

The need has long existed for this type of material in the pet bird industry. Although there is a limited amount of material on the keeping and breeding of pet birds, it is directed primarily towards the hobbyist, and there is absolutely no viable material on the marketing of pet birds that I am aware of. This book is different. It is written for the person who wishes to make a good income, while building a solid business at home, doing something that they truly enjoy. The utilization of the ideas and techniques in this book will mean that you are learning from other people's experiences. This can dramatically shorten your learning process, and that is the only practical way to grow, as it is too frustrating, too time consuming and far too costly to learn everything from personal experience. By adhering to the techniques outlined in the following pages, you will capitalize on our 25 years of experience in successfully breeding, buying, selling and shipping of exotic birds for profit.

While it is a little known fact, the commercial production of pet birds is a well established business that is well over 100 years old. It has thrived and grown right through the great depression, many recessions, and numerous wars. Now, it is poised to become even stronger in the future. As a result of the Wild Bird Conservation act passed by Congress, the USDA now limits the amounts and types of wild caught birds that can be imported into the United States. This has created a never-ending demand for people to raise domestically bred pet birds.

Whether it is your goal to make $2,000 monthly on a part-time basis, or $50,000 yearly on a full-time basis, I'll show you how to breed the four most popular types of pet birds and where to sell them. Once you get the feel for the business, you may elect to become a nationwide wholesale distributor of pet birds and go for the really serious income north of $100,000 annually. I'll show you how and where to build those markets.

Will Rogers once made the observation that, "In order to succeed, you must know what you are doing, like what you are doing, and believe in what you are doing." It is estimated that almost 80% of the working population reluctantly go to work every day. It's not that they are a lazy people. They are simply uninspired. They either don't like their working environment or they don't like what they are doing. And that is a tragedy if you live in America. The amount of immigrants, many of which are uneducated, that come to our country flat broke and in a few short years become successful business people, is staggering. The way you see life will largely determine what you get out of it, and they see life in America as one really big opportunity. This book will make you aware of the great opportunities to make some extremely good money, while being self-employed in an enjoyable occupation in the pet bird business. Very few people lack the ability to succeed in this business if they are willing to work at it. It's simply not a hard business to learn.

Since this book covers the breeding and raising of a number of different species of pet birds, the reader may find a small amount of repetition in certain topics that may share common ground with the different species of birds. However, it is my belief that it is very important to include the significant points in each chapter that are needed to help you achieve success with each separate species of bird. Some readers may show interest in and read about only one particular type of bird, therefore missing vital information.

I say with all candor and with respect to others that the methods expressed in this book are not the only means by which you can achieve success in this field, but represent the methods that have proven by far to work the best for us. Just as there are many different roads that lead from point A to point B, there are many different ways to breed and market birds. However, some roads are shorter and have less bumps than others. If someone will map you a road that is shorter with less bumps, you will normally arrive at your destination far ahead of the crowd. It is my hope that this book will provide you with that map.

Parakeets remain the most popular pet birds of all time

Chapter 1

Raising Exotic Birds for Profit

**Two "American Dream" success stories
made possible by pet birds...**

In 1974 my wife and I were both working at public jobs; she as a seamstress in a clothing factory and I was driving a potato chip truck. We had been married for several ears and knew that at some point we would like to have a family, and both of us wanted her to be able to stay at home and raise the kids. However, my job on the potato chip truck had not exactly put us in the upper tax bracket, so we desperately needed her income if we were to take on the additional expense of raising a family. I began to look for things that she could do at home to supplement our income, but it seemed like virtually everything I researched was in some way some type of a scam or a rip-off, as someone was always attempting to sell me a bill of goods of some description in some way or another.

I knew of two different people in my area that were raising parakeets in small buildings in their backyard. Both had been doing it for a number of years and appeared to me to be doing pretty good at it, since each of them had expanded during that time. A visit with them was encouraging, and after several months of what I considered to be some pretty in-depth research, we decided that it was in fact a legitimate business; and being animal lovers, we thought it would not only be profitable, but also fun. We started our bird business on a part-time basis in our backyard in 1975 with a small 12x18-ft. building that I built myself. By 1976 my wife was doing well enough with the project that we decided to expand the business. We built several more small buildings and the birds continued to do well and she was soon able to quit her job and take care of the birds on a full-time basis. In 1977 our first child was born and my wife was now the stay at home mom that she had always wanted to be.

By 1978 the business was booming and she was making much more money than I was. We now began to more fully realize the potential of the bird business. Seeing the opportunity for even more expansion, I quit the potato chip route and we both went full- time with the birds. We expanded into other varieties of pet birds and the business was simply so good that we could not keep up with the demand. At that point, I began to recruit others to raise birds for us and we soon became a nationwide wholesale distributor of pet birds by 1980. Our business was still a mom and pop operation with the mom now also raising our two boys. During the next 10 years we remained a mom and pop operation with no employees, finally hiring a single employee in 1990. I hasten to add that the year we started, 1975, the U.S. economy went into a recession. The economy also experienced other recessions in 1980 and 1982, and another in 1991 as well as the Gulf War in 1991. Throughout it all, the pet business boomed. We continued to experience explosive growth and in 2000, after 25 years in the business, after having sold around a million birds, at the age of 50 we sold our business and retired to the Texas hill country. The pet business truly allowed us to live "The American Dream" of owning our own successful business. Although ours is a success story, it pales in comparison to the following.

The following is by far the most amazing success story I know of in the pet industry. It is the story of Max Stern. Max was a German immigrant who came to the U.S. in 1926 looking for the freedom and unlimited opportunity that America offered. He brought with him 5,000 singing canaries. Soon after arriving in New York with his canaries, although he could not speak English, he was able to sell them to the Wannamaker Department Store at Astor Place in Manhattan. Max then returned to Germany many more times to bring back more canaries. His customers soon included Sears Roebuck, F.W. Woolworth, W.T. Grants, S.S. Kresge, as well as others. By 1932 Max was the largest livestock importer in the country. He decided to expand the business by entering into the packaged bird feed business. That was the beginning of the Hartz Mountain product line. If you are not familiar with the name Max Stern, you are surely familiar with some of his products. By 1980 Hartz Mountain products were sold in more than 40,000 U.S. and Canadian retail outlets. They were pioneers in the sale of millions of canaries, parakeets, finches, cockatiels, hamsters, tropical fish and supplies in variety stores throughout the United States. In 1959 Max's son, Leonard, joined the company and rapidly expanded their products to include the dog and cat supplies. One of their most widely known products is the Hartz Mountain flea and tick collar. Under his leadership, the company continued to grow at a remarkable pace. Max Stern, the founder, passed away in 1982.

In December 2000, after 75 years as a "family business", the Stern family sold Hartz Mountain to a private investment firm specializing in buyouts of middle-sized growth companies. In 1982, Forbes magazine began publishing the Forbes 400-the names of the 400 wealthiest people in the U.S. The September 1982 issue listed Leonard Stern's net worth in excess of $500 million. Including real estate, the October 1988 issue of Forbes listed Mr. Stern's net worth at $1.3 BILLION. That is absolutely remarkable when you consider that it all started with some canaries in 1926. The Stern family TRULY has lived "The American Dream" as a result of the pet business. I hasten to add that Max Stern started the business right before the Great Depression and it not only survived, but grew by leaps and bounds through the depression, many recessions, as well as several major wars. It is safe to say that our country's love for pets has not been slowed by bad economic times.

Although the Stern family success story would surely be hard, if not down right impossible to duplicate, the first story, my story, is not that hard to repeat. The following chapters guide you through the necessary steps needed to become successful not only in raising the four most popular types of pet birds, but where the markets are, and if you so desire, how to successfully build a nationwide wholesale distributorship of pet birds that has a huge income potential.

Please take me serious when I say that the pet bird business is not some fly by night, get rich quick scheme. The commercial pet bird business is a legitimate business that has a good, solid, proven long term history behind it, and one that, if you are willing to work at it, can reward you very handsomely for your efforts.

I have known many different people from various walks of life who, for different reasons, have gotten into the bird business and have done extremely well. As a wholesale distributor of pet birds, we have bought hundreds of thousands of birds from farmers, ranchers, firemen, contractors, beauticians, doctors, bankers, teachers, truck drivers, airline pilots, engineers, preachers, newspaper journalist, etc., as well as many retirees and stay at home moms. I personally know several people who have became very wealthy as a result of being in the bird business. But I want to again stress that this is not a get rich quick scheme, but that it is an enjoyable occupation that you can start part-time and quickly build to the point of becoming an extremely profitable full-time business if you so desire. It's a proven fact that there have been, there are, and there will continue to be many people making very good money in the pet bird business. It's simply a matter of recognizing the opportunity.

I believe it is possible for just about anyone to succeed in this business if they posses these two things-the love of animals and a sincere desire to work for yourself. A person must love or enjoy what they do if they are to truly succeed in whatever it is they are doing. Personally, I don't like working on an automobile. Don't like it at all. Not even a little. I don't like the oil and grease of the motor, the busted knuckles you get when a wrench slips off, or going to find the wrench after frustration causes me to throw it. I can do it, but I just don't like to. Therefore, I don't think that I would ever be very successful running my own business as a mechanic, but there are others who love working on automobiles and do very well at it. They are the ones who stand the better chance of being successful in that business, not me. I believe the same is true in the bird business. If you don't like birds, animals, or nature, you probably won't be very successful in this industry. Money is a great motivator, but I really think that it takes more than that to succeed in this business or any other. But if you enjoy birds and animals and have a strong desire to own your own business, then you owe it to yourself to fully investigate the pet bird business. You will find that it offers a tremendous opportunity to become self-employed and set your own income level, as either a part-time or full-time breeder or wholesale distributor of parakeets, cockatiels, lovebirds and finches.

Pet Industry Facts

1. Our love and demand for pets is clearly indicated by the growth in spending that is seen each year in the pet industry. U. S. consumers are spending more on pets than ever before. In 1998 Americans spent $23 billion in the pet industry. The American Pet Products Manufacturers Association estimates that in 2003 we will spend $31 billion on pets and pet products.
2. Currently, 62% of U.S. households own a pet compared with 56% in 1988 and 47% of all households in the U.S. own more than one type of pet.
3. 7% of all households own a bird of some type.
4. In 1990 there were 11 million pet birds living in U.S. households. That number had grown to over 20 million by 2000, with some estimates as high as 50 million by the year 2010.
5. One-third of the pet owners consider their pets as children or as family members.
6. In the past 10 years the number of households owning a pet has increased by 10 million, indicating exceptionally strong growth in pet ownership.

Birds are an extremely popular pet with both children and older, retired people alike. With a growing population of children as well as an unprecedented amount of baby boomers approaching retirement age, the demand is huge for people to raise certain types of the most popular breeds of exotic birds. It is a proven fact that people are

The greatest backyard business ever!

going to have their pets; they always have, and they always will, regardless of economic times. The bird business thrived right through the Great Depression of 1929, as well as the numerous recessions we have experienced since then. Some of our best growth years in this business were actually during years that our economy was experiencing recession. History has shown that during economic slowdowns consumers will cut back spending on the large ticket items, but they will continue to spend on small dollar items that are either entertaining or amusing. The bottom line is that our country has an enormous appetite for pets and there is a strong demand for people to raise certain types of them.

So Why Choose Birds?

For many years, wild caught birds competed with domestic bred birds in the pet business. As a result of the Wild Bird Conservation Act passed by Congress, the United States Department of Agriculture now limits the amount and types of birds that can be imported into the United States from other countries. Other than a select few for zoological and certain other purposes, the importation of wild caught birds from other countries has been gradually and progressively phased out and is now to the point that it is virtually non-existent, and will remain so in the future. This has created an even greater demand for domestically bred pet birds.

However, the importation limitations were implemented many years after we had entered the business. I would like to mention some other things that contributed to the reason why we got into the business and I think that they are still very valid reasons today. These are reasons that you will want to strongly consider when making your decision.

- With over 8,000 individual retail pet shops as well as countless other outlets in the U.S. selling pet birds, the need for a steady supply of birds is strong. Think about it. Where do those birds come from? With imports a thing of the past, there is a steady demand for people to breed birds to supply the pet industry with the millions of birds annually sold.

- Raising birds is something that can be started on a small scale for a minimum start up cost.
- People have successfully raised birds in anything from a basement in their house, to a patio, a portable building, mobile home or a custom built commercial size building. A portable building in the backyard is a very popular and inexpensive method that many people choose.
- High profit margins are attainable on the offspring sold. You sell them as youngsters.
- Raising birds requires no high-powered education, only common sense.
- You don't need any incubators or other high priced equipment- the adult birds raise their own babies in their own nestboxes.
- It can be successfully done in all 50 states, regardless of the size of your town or location, as long as you are located within a 4 to 5 hour drive of a major airport. That will allow you to ship any excess birds by airfreight to anywhere in the U.S. This business is simply not dependent upon your location, as it is a nation wide business. We didn't sell ANY birds in our hometown of Corsicana, Texas.
- It can be done in town or country, indoors or out, depending upon the layout of your facilities.
- It requires a minimum amount of time and effort, depending of course, on the size of your operation. It can easily be started on a part-time basis, devoting a few hours a week, and grown into a full-time business.
- Parakeets are by far the most popular of all pet birds, followed by cockatiels, lovebirds and finches. They are virtually odorless and attract no flies, fleas, or other insects. The same cannot be said for other forms of livestock.
- Best of all, it can be extremely profitable. Many part-time breeders make from $500 to $2,000 monthly, while a full-time breeder can make upwards of $50,000 yearly, and a breeder that is also a wholesale distributor of birds can make in excess of $100,000 yearly.

The greatest backyard business ever!

The pet bird business is not dominated by any large conglomerate, as are many other businesses. While breeding exotic birds can be easy and very profitable, it is something that requires the dedication and watchful eye of someone that actually loves and enjoys working with birds and animals. It is easy to hire workers to clean cages and put out feed, but most commercial bird raisers choose to have a breeding operation that they can oversee and manage themselves, thus, practically all of the birds that supply the pet bird industry today are bred by mom and pop operations throughout the country.

Parakeets, cockatiels, lovebirds and finches have relatively short life spans. That in itself creates a never ending demand for them. Consider the fact that many children will have several different parakeets or other birds during their childhood years, and the fact that there are 281 million people in our country says that there is a tremendous need for people to raise pet birds to satisfy the demands of both the young and old alike.

Another positive factor that we found extremely attractive was the fact that birds are sold the by the head and not by the pound. Having been raised on a farm, I knew all too well that many times all of your profits would evaporate because you had to pump so much feed into an animal before it reached a marketable weight or age. The birds appealed to us because they could be sold when they were babies, and you just didn't have that much expense in them. And perhaps one of the things that my wife liked most of all about the birds was the fact that they were virtually odorless. As a wholesale distributor, the building where we housed the birds prior to shipment measured 24 ft. x 56 ft. At times, we would have between 3000-4000 birds in that building and there just wasn't any offensive odor at all. Such is not the case with almost any other type of animal. You just cannot put that many dogs, cats, hamsters, rabbits, mice or any other animal in a building that size and not have an odor problem. The lack of odor means that you can raise them in town as well as the country. We also never had a problem with insects.

A note worth mentioning at this point-the parakeet, zebra finch, cockatiel and lovebird diet consist mainly of a dry seed mixture, and they consume very little water. Therefore, the birds droppings are almost dry by the time they hit the ground. Some types of exotic birds require a lot of fruit and vegetables in their diet, and therefore have a much looser stool, which can attract flies and cause odor problems. Be advised that I am not discouraging the breeding of other types of birds, as many people do extremely well with them, its just that we were personally attracted to the parakeets, cockatiels, finches and lovebirds for the above mentioned reasons.

Raising birds is something that almost anyone can do, male or female, young or old, as there is nothing physically demanding about it. As I stated earlier, my wife was the one who started raising parakeets, and it quickly grew into a business that provided the opportunity for me to quit my job and join her in a business that rewarded us beyond all expectations. The bird business allowed us the opportunity to work at home, make an extremely good living, send our boys through college, and take an early retirement. The bird business is not a fly by night scheme or fad. It has stood the test of time. It has been around since the turn of the century, through good times and bad, and its future looks as bright as ever.

We started our business on a part-time basis in 1975 with the small building in the right side of this picture. Within 3 years we were making a good living on a full time basis in the pet bird business.

Chapter 2

Why Start With Parakeets, Cockatiels, Lovebirds Or Zebra Finches?

As you begin to realize the opportunities and potential that the exotic bird business offers and you consider getting into it, your next decision must be to decide which types of birds to breed.

I will explain some of the pros and cons of the different species of pet birds. There is one thing you must know about pet birds compared to some of the other types of birds and fowl. The pet birds we refer to hatch and raise their own babies, whereas some birds such as quail or pheasants, upon hatching are able to run around and eat, drink, and fend for themselves from day one. Not so with most exotic birds. They are like a little puppy or kitten. They come into the world with their eyes closed and are totally helpless and must be fed by their parents until such time as they are able to fly out of the nest and survive on their own. Usually, both parents help in the rearing process and that is why you must breed pairs of birds. They are not like chickens, where you can have one rooster and a whole flock of hens.

In choosing which species of birds to begin with, quite simply, you should start with the birds that are the easiest to breed and have the biggest demand. Without a doubt the easiest to breed and sell are the parakeet, finch, cockatiel and lovebirds.

I believe the parakeet to be by far the most popular pet bird of all time. They are hardy little birds that come in a rainbow of different colors, are intelligent and entertaining, and they love affection and human companionship. They can also be taught to talk and do tricks. These are just a few of the things that make them so popular with both kids and adults alike. When you take into consideration that there is currently an estimated 20 million pet birds in the United

The greatest backyard business ever!

States and that our human population is growing, it stands to reason that the demand for this popular little bird will continue. Parakeets are easy to distinguish between the sexes, quite prolific, usually make very good parents and will reach sexual maturity at an early age. Parakeets probably accounts for somewhere around 60 to 75 percent of all the birds sold in the pet industry.

Single Breeding

Parakeets have been providing fun and entertainment for children for generations.

Finches are just as easy to breed as parakeets, perhaps easier. Throughout this book the species of finch that I primarily refer to is the zebra finch. There are many different species of finches, some which bring very good prices, but most are usually more difficult to breed and market than the zebra finch. The zebra finch is one of the smaller birds of the finch family, but it is one of the most prolific. Zebras are easy to distinguish between the sexes and they also make very good parent birds. They tend to reach sexual maturity at a very early age. Zebra finches are social birds and do best in a colony situation. They do not, however have the personalities that parakeets and cockatiels have, and consequently do not make the best personal pets. Even though zebra finches have been bred in captivity for many, many

Colony Breeding

years, they have retained much of the behavior of their wild Australian counterparts. Although they will not attach themselves to their owners and become as hand tame as parakeets and cockatiels do, they are nevertheless great little birds to keep and observe. They should be kept in pairs or small groups; therefore, most people that have them have more than one. Hence, the demand for finches is good.

Next is the cockatiel. It is the larger of these four types of exotic birds and usually the most expensive. It is not difficult to distinguish between the sexes and is fairly prolific. Cockatiels come in several different colors, although not nearly as many as the parakeet. The cockatiel is normally a good parent bird and tends to raises its babies quite well. Like the parakeet, the cockatiel can be taught to do tricks and talk, and they frequently become very attached to their owners. Because of its higher price, both for the bird and the cage required to house it, the retail demand is not nearly as strong for the cockatiel as it is for the parakeet.

Lovebirds are perhaps the most difficult to breed of the four species of birds recommended for the beginner to choose from. They are much more difficult to sex and with the exception of the peachface, are not usually as prolific as the

The greatest backyard business ever!

other species we have discussed. There are a number of different types of lovebirds, but by far the most common is the peachface, followed by the blackmask, bluemask and fisher. The peachface has several different color mutations which almost always bring premium prices. The peachface are the more prolific of the group and would be the recommended choice of the lovebird family for the beginner to start with. They are very hardy little birds and can be bred in either cages or colonies, but seem to do better in colonies. Lovebirds are absolutely beautiful little birds, but they cannot be taught to talk and therefore do not enjoy quite as much popularity as do parakeets and cockatiels.

I believe when making the decision as to what species of birds to start with, it should be based on your own personal preference. I do believe, however, that you should start with one of these four, which are the simplest to raise. You may, after time, decide to try raising some of the other larger Psittacine birds (birds with hookbills) such as the parrots, macaws, cockatoos, conures, etc., or some of the other smaller types of Passerine birds (songbird, finch- type birds with straight bills) such as society finches, lady gould finches, canaries, etc. Although these can surely be profitable to raise, they are much more difficult to breed and in some cases more difficult to market.

I have a real estate license. Overall, it is much more difficult to market and sell a 6 bedroom, 6 bath, 4 car garage house than it is to market and sell a 3 bedroom, 2 bath, 2 car garage house. Two reasons why. First and foremost, more people can afford a 3/2/2 house than can afford a 6/6/4 house. Second, most people don't want the larger house because of the required upkeep and other work associated with it even if they could afford it. Hence, the demand just isn't there for the larger more expensive house that there is for the less expensive house. Builders have figured that out and have met the demands of the market place by building mostly 3/2/2 houses.

The absolute same thing is true in dealing with birds. More people can afford a parakeet, cockatiel or finch than can afford a macaw, cockatoo or amazon parrot. As a producer, you must respond to the demands of the marketplace and produce what sells best.

Another reason why the beginner should not start with the larger birds is that many of them are dimorphic, meaning that you cannot visually distinguish the difference between the sexes. For many of these larger birds the sex can only be determined by having them surgically sexed or by testing the bird's DNA, both of which are costly. In addition to being difficult to sex, most of the larger birds do not reach sexual maturity until they are several years old, and even then, they may sit there many more years without bonding to the mate that you have chosen for them. Then, if and when they do breed, in order to bring the best price, the chicks must to be taken from the nest, hand fed and raised so they will be very tame when they are purchased as a pet. Few people want a large bird that is not tame, therefore, most of the chicks simply must be hand fed, which requires being done every few hours, 7 days a week, until they reach a marketable age.

Next is the noise factor. I believe the big birds would be difficult to raise in town on a very large scale. There is a blue and gold macaw that lives down the street from me. Most of the year his owner keeps him outdoors in his cage. He doesn't bother me at all, in fact, I enjoy listing to him, especially when he goes to talking and laughing. But the fact that he lives down the street from me and I can hear him up the hill where I live, tells me that if there were a number of birds as vocal as him living down there, neighbors would probably be complaining about the noise. While out jogging, I have heard him screaming almost a half mile away. I have been fortunate enough to have visited some of the largest exotic bird farms in the country, and I can tell you from experience that the larger birds can get pretty noisy. Although the prices are much higher, with many of them bringing into the thousands of dollars for a single hand fed baby, they are generally not the best birds for the beginner to breed and raise. I don't mean to sound discouraging on the larger birds. I know of some who have done very well breeding the larger hookbills, I just

The greatest backyard business ever!

wouldn't advise starting out with them. If after you start with the smaller birds and find that you like the business and feel that you would like to breed the larger birds, then by all means go for it.

That brings up another point. After you get into the bird business, you will, no doubt, from time to time become aware of other opportunities regarding other types of exotic animals. During our 25 years in the business, in addition to birds, we have had many other types of critters. We've had turtles and reptiles, ostrich, emu, potbelly pigs, miniature donkeys, and an assortment of different types of exotic deer and antelope. Virtually every square foot of our 20 acres was an income producer of some description. At times, there was some very good money to be made with some of the aforementioned birds and animals, and at times there wasn't. As a wholesale distributor, we had many people who raised birds for us, and, as is only natural, many of those people would become curious of the other types of birds and animals we were working with. Invariably, they would begin to question us as to how hard they were to breed and how much money could you make raising and selling them. I guess its just human nature that the grass always appears greener on the other side of the fence.

As I noted earlier, at times you could make a lot of money with some of those other types of birds and animals. From the mid 1980's to the mid 90's, the exotic animal business experienced a tremendous boom. Many of these exotics, such as the potbelly pigs, hedgehogs, etc. were just fads. I'm sorry, I just don't think pigs make very good house pets. Apparently, a lot of other people felt the same way as the pig craze didn't fly for very long, although a lot of money could have been made if you had gotten into the business at the right time. Much of the exotic animal boom of the 80's and 90's is attributed to the fact that these animals were going through a breeder's market. A breeder's market being defined as a market whereby there is a limited supply of birds or animals that are available for breeding purposes and a strong demand exists for more. Most all types of animals go through a breeder's market at some point in time.

Shorthorn cattle were first imported from Great Britain into the United States in 1623. The importers didn't eat those first few, but for years a few people enjoyed the inflated prices of a breeder's market. Sometimes, breeder's markets can last for many, many years. As the number of animals multiplied, breeder's market prices dropped until they finally stabilized at the true market value of the animal. In the case of the shorthorn cattle, the true market price of the animal is the price the consumer is willing to pay for the meat in the grocery store.

Well, since the grass invariably almost always looks greener on the other side of the fence, to keep the people who were already raising birds for us from being too quick to jump that fence, I would caution them that those other birds and animals were as yet unproven in their markets but that the parakeets, cockatiels, lovebirds and finches that they were breeding had a proven market that would continue to be there long after some of those other fads had passed. Such has been the case.

Other exotic animal markets have come and gone, but pet birds such as parakeets, cockatiels, lovebirds and zebra finches have stood

The greatest backyard business ever!

the test of time. The fact remains, there have been, there are, and there will continue to be many people making very good money in the pet bird business.

Chapter 3

Prices are quoted for Volume Selling

Can I Make A Profit Breeding Birds?

Absolutely. Breeding birds can be a very profitably business if done correctly. However, the pet bird business is no different than most other types of businesses in that it has its ups and downs. But the people who go into the bird breeding business and take it seriously, and manage their breeding operation properly, usually wind up doing very well. Many of them start part-time and in a few years have grown their business into a full-time operation, usually branching out and breeding several different types of birds. This is my recommendation; start small, make sure you enjoy the business, and then grow larger if that is your goal.

It is a good idea to diversify as you grow, since in some years parakeets may be down in price and cockatiels prices may be up. Next year, cockatiels may be down in price and parakeets or finches may be in short supply, thus bringing a premium price. You will find that prices do vary from year to year and from species to species. Most farmers don't plant just one crop. They diversify and take advantage of different crops and price swings. Birds are no different. It will pay you well to diversify, especially if you intend to be in the business full-time.

There are a number of different ways in which you can market your birds. Each can make a considerable amount of difference in the price you receive and we will discuss them in detail a little later, but the following prices are what you might expect a wholesale bird buyer to pay you for your birds. Parakeets prices will usually range from between $3.50 to $4.50 per bird. Cockatiel prices range from between $14 to $22 per bird, lovebirds from $12 to $26 and finches from $2.50 to $4.00 per bird. These are somewhat normal price

The greatest backyard business ever!   35

ranges. I have seen the wholesale prices on parakeets as high as $6.00 each and as much as $30.00 on cockatiels and lovebirds. However, they usually don't stay at those prices very long and it is wise not to use inflated prices when establishing your business plan.

Its best to use average prices, maybe even with a bias towards the low side when making your projections. By doing so, if prices surprise you to the upside, it's just gravy on your platter. Larger breeders will almost always sell their birds at wholesale prices, usually to a bird buyer. But many smaller breeders will sometimes elect to sell a portion or all of their birds through other means at much higher prices. We will cover other avenues of selling birds a little later in the book.

Parakeets

A pair of parakeets will produce an average of 4 to 6 babies per clutch and can have from 4 to 6 clutches per year. If the conditions are right, they will lay one clutch right after another, all year long. The most babies I have ever had a pair to produce in a year was 38. You can easily see that there is a wide range in the number of offspring that a pair of parakeets will produce in a year, just as there is a wide range in the prices they will bring.

Although it will vary from year to year, depending on the cost of feed, the cost to produce a parakeet will usually range from between $.75 to $1.00 per bird, not counting your labor or the cost of your building. Using the average wholesale price of $4.00 per parakeet, less an average of $.85 to produce it, you would have an average profit of $3.15 per bird. Using those profit margins, you can use the figures below to give you an idea of the number of birds you might need to produce in order to reach the income you desire. That will in turn give you an idea of the size facility you will need for your bird breeding business.

Average estimated wholesale price per parakeet	$4.00
Average estimated cost to produce a parakeet	- .85
Average estimated profit per bird	$3.15

*The following calculations are based
on an average estimated profit of $3.15 per bird.*

100 pair x 10 babies per pair=1,000 babies x $3.15=$3,150
100 pair x 20 babies per pair=2,000 babies x $3.15=$6,300
100 pair x 30 babies per pair=3,000 babies x $3.15=$9,450

250 pair x 10 babies per pair=2,500 babies x $3.15=$7,875
250 pair x 20 babies per pair =5,000 babies x $3.15=$15,750
250 pair x 30 babies per pair =7,500 babies x $3.15=$23,625

500 pair x 10 babies per pair =5,000 babies x $3.15=$15,750
500 pair x 20 babies per pair =10,000 babies x $3.15=$31,500
500 pair x 30 babies per pair =15,000 babies x $3.15=$47,250

While this may seem like a wide variance in the amount of offspring per pair per year, there actually can be that much of a range, depending on the age and quality of your birds, as well as whether or not you are cage breeding or colony breeding. An average of 25 to 30 chicks per pair per year is not at all unrealistic with good birds in a cage breeding operation, although I would encourage the use of the lower figures when projecting future income for your business plan.

The above prices are based on baby birds from 6 to about 12 weeks of age. Baby birds are easier to train than adult birds, hence the demand is always much greater for babies than it is for adults. This usually holds true for almost any type of bird or animal that is used for a pet. Adult parakeets never bring a very good price, with the wholesale price usually being somewhere in the neighborhood of $1 to $1.50 each.

You must bear in mind that these are only estimated averages and that things can and will change from year to year. But you can clearly see that the potential is there to earn some very good money breeding parakeets. One of the keys to increased profitability is to increase your annual production on a per pair basis. Since some costs such as utilities and building expenses are fixed and will remain the same over time, if you can increase your production by only 2 babies per pair per year, it will have a huge impact on your bottom line if you have quite a few pair. Although parakeets can live for up to 8 or 10 years, and will continue to produce young for almost as long, their production goes to falling off after about 3 years and at that point, if you want to maximize your profits, you should replace them with young birds. However, that is done on a gradual basis and can be done in such a manner so as not to effect your yearly production very much. We will cover that a little later in the book.

Cockatiels

Cockatiels are not usually quite as prolific as parakeets. They will normally have from 4 to 6 babies per clutch, although they can have up to 8 or 9, but usually only have 3 to 4 clutches per year. Cockatiels also have a much wider price range than parakeets do. The normal color of a cockatiel is considered to be gray. As a general rule, any color other than gray will bring a better price. Albino and pied cockatiels usually bring the best prices, and for the most part are just as easy to raise. Just as we did with the parakeets, we will use the average price that you could expect to receive from a wholesaler to calculate some average income estimates from breeding cockatiels. The average wholesale prices that a normal gray cockatiel should be expected to bring will range from $14 to $18 each, and the range of pied and albino cockatiels is usually somewhere between $18 to $22 each. I have seen albinos and pieds bring as much as $30 each, and normal grays as much as $21 each, but again, you are by far better to use the lower averages when making a profit projection. You should be able to produce a cockatiel for around $3, not including labor or building cost. Using the above averages, we can now make some income estimations.

Average estimated wholesale price for a normal cockatiel $16.00
Average estimated cost to produce a normal cockatiel -3.00
Average estimated profit per bird $13.00

The following calculations are based on an average estimated profit of $13.00 per bird.

10 pair x 10 babies per pair=100 babies x $13.00=$1,300
10 pair x 15 babies per pair=150 babies x $13.00=$1,950
10 pair x 20 babies per pair=200 babies x $13.00=$2,600

50 pair x 10 babies per pair=500 babies x $13.00=$6,500
50 pair x 15 babies per pair=750 babies x $13.00=$9,750
50 pair x 20 babies per pair=1000 babies x $13.00=$13,000

100 pair x 15 babies per pair=1500 babies x $13.00=$19,500

Average estimated wholesale price for a pied or albino cockatiel	$20.00
Average estimated cost to produce a pied or an albino cockatiel	-3.00
Average estimated profit per bird.	$17.00

10 pair x 10 babies per pair=100 babies x $17.00=$1,700
10 pair x 15 babies per pair=150 babies x $17.00=$2,550
10 pair x 20 babies per pair=200 babies x $17.00=$3,400

50 pair x 10 babies per pair=500 babies x $17.00=$8,500
50 pair x 15 babies per pair=750 babies x $17.00=$12,750
50 pair x 20 babies per pair=1000 babies x $17.00=$17,000

100 pair x 15 babies per pair=1500 babies x $17.00=$25,500

You might look at the above comparison between parakeets and cockatiels and figure that you could make much more money breeding cockatiels than you could breeding parakeets. That is not necessarily the case. Cockatiels require a lot more space per bird than do parakeets. There are, however, many people that simply do much better breeding cockatiels than they do breeding parakeets. It just boils down to your own personal preference. It is usually best to at least consider diversifying, and maybe raise some of each.

Cockatiels generally have a lifespan of around 15 to 20 years, but their production will reach its peak long before then. When the production goes to declining in the bird breeding business, it is time to replace the breed stock with younger, more productive birds. This is usually around 6 to 10 years in the case of the cockatiels.

Although the majority of pet shops would rather buy baby cockatiels because they are easier to train than adult birds are, the price is usually somewhere about the same for adults as it is for babies. I suppose that is because the older cockatiels are usually more colorful than the youngsters.

Lovebirds

Lovebirds, with the possible exception of the peachface lovebird, are a little more difficult to breed than are the parakeets and cockatiels. If you are considering breeding lovebirds, by all means start out with the peachface. They are usually more prolific and easier to raise than are the blackmask, bluemask or fisher lovebirds. Peachface will generally have from 3 to 7 chicks per clutch, averaging around 4, and will normally have from 3 to 5 clutches per year. The peachface has several different color mutations and prices vary accordingly to the scarcity of the different mutations. Prices that a normal peachface lovebird could be expected to bring range from $12 to $18 each. Pied peachface can range from $20 to $26 each and lutino peachface can range from $22 to $28 each. As you can see, the different colors do most definitely make a difference regarding the prices lovebirds will bring. The cost to produce a peachface lovebird is usually somewhere around $2.50, not including your labor or building costs. Using these figures we can now calculate some profit estimations.

Ave. estimated wholesale price
 for a normal peachface lovebird $15.00
Average estimated cost to produce
 a normal peachface lovebird   -2.50
Average estimated profit per bird $12.50

The following is based on an average estimated profit of $12.50 per bird

10 pair x 10 babies per pair=100 babies x $12.50=$1,250
10 pair x 15 babies per pair=150 babies x $12.50=$1,875
10 pair x 20 babies per pair=200 babies x $12.50=$2,500

50 pair x 10 babies per pair=500 babies x $12.50=$6,250
50 pair x 15 babies per pair=750 babies x $12.50=$9,375
50 pair x 20 babies per pair=1000 babies x $12.50=$12,500

Average estimated wholesale price
 for a pied or lutino peachface lovebird $23.00
Average estimated cost to produce
 pied or lutino peachface lovebird   - 2.50
Average estimated profit per bird $20.50

10 pair x 10 babies per pair=100 babies x $20.50=$2,050
10 pair x 15 babies per pair=150 babies x $20.50=$3,075
10 pair x 20 babies per pair=200 babies x $20.50=$4,100

50 pair x 10 babies per pair=500 babies x $20.50=$10,250
50 pair x 15 babies per pair=750 babies x $20.50=$15,375
50 pair x 20 babies per pair=1000 babies x $20.50=$20,500

As you can clearly see, there is money to be made breeding lovebirds, but please remember that these figures represent averages, both on prices and production. I have not included prices on blackmask, bluemask or fisher lovebirds, but they will usually bring somewhere around the same prices as the pied peachface do. One might look at these figures and conclude that if they had 250 pair of pied or lutino peachface lovebirds and they averaged 20 babies per pair that they could make in excess of $100,000 yearly by breeding them. While I suppose that would be possible, it surely would be exceptional. But I do know a breeder who specialized in breeding lovebirds and he would sometimes produced in the neighborhood of 3,000 to 5,000 lovebirds yearly, and for years he even held down a full-time job while doing so. His was a family run business and he knew exactly what he was doing. We bought birds from him for many years before we sold our business and he produced some of the best peachface lovebirds that I have ever seen.

Lovebirds have a life span similar to that of the cockatiel, around 15 to 20 years, but production will normally begin to fall off when they are around 6 or 7 years old. For maximum production you should replace your lovebirds when they reach that age, or whenever you notice their yearly production slowing down.

Zebra Finches

Zebra finches are very good breeders and are usually quite profitable to raise. They will generally have 4 to 6 babies per clutch and can have from 4 to 6 clutches per year, sometimes more. The wholesale price of zebra finches will normally range from $2.50 to $4.00 per bird, and the cost to produce a zebra finch is usually around $.60, not including labor or building costs. Using those average estimated figures, we can now make some profit projections from breeding zebra finches.

Average estimated wholesale price for a zebra finch	$3.25
Average estimated cost to produce a zebra finch	-.60
Average estimated profit per bird	$2.65

The following is based on an average estimated profit of $2.65 per bird.

100 pair x 10 babies per pair=1,000 babies x $2.65=$2,650
100 pair x 15 babies per pair=1,500 babies x $2.65=$3,975
100 pair x 20 babies per pair=2,000 babies x $2.65=$5,300
300 pair x 10 babies per pair=3,000 babies x $2.65=$7,950
300 pair x 15 babies per pair=4,500 babies x $2.65=$11,925
300 pair x 20 babies per pair=6,000 babies x $2.65=$15,900

500 pair x 10 babies per pair=5,000 babies x $2.65=$13,250
500 pair x 15 babies per pair=7,500 babies x $2.65=$19,875
500 pair x 20 babies per pair=10,000 babies x $2.65=$26,500

Zebra finches have a shorter life span than do parakeets, cockatiels or lovebirds. With a heart rate between 850 to 1200 beats per minute, they are very active little birds with a very high metabolism and are hardly ever still for very long. Although they can live up to about 6 years or so, they usually do not produce well for more than 3 years.

Adult zebra finches are much more colorful than the youngsters are, and since finches are not considered to be a very trainable bird, most pet shops would just as soon to have an adult zebra finch as a baby. Therefore the price is usually the same for either.

In deciding what species of birds you want to breed, it is important to consider the necessary space requirements for each species. Generally, the larger the bird is, the more space it will require to house and breed the birds. Space requirements will be covered in more detail later in the book.

In using the above figures to project income from breeding these different types of birds, remember these are estimated yearly averages that can and will vary from year to year. However, these averages have been a fairly good rule of thumb in the past and will most likely be so in the future, but I would strongly encourage you to use the low end of all ranges when making your estimated income projections. Better to be surprised to the upside than the downside.

Farmers and ranchers alike must use historical prices to project their future prices. It is no different in the bird business. One thing to keep in mind is that these above figures represent the various wholesale prices that have been paid in the past for selling these different types of birds in <u>volume</u>. If a person is not breeding birds in large volumes, they may not wish to sell to a wholesaler and they can often receive prices that are considerably higher. We cover that a little later in the book.

In comparing raising birds to raising other types of livestock, I have a story that I would like to share. A number of years ago, a gentleman by the name of Lano Barron came by our place gathering information on raising birds. He was a couple of years away from retirement, and was looking for something else to do when he retired. He was a rancher and a professor of agriculture at Navarro College in Corsicana, Texas, as well as a math teacher. He held a doctorate degree. If there ever was a numbers cruncher, it was Dr. Barron. He thoroughly put the pencil to things. He built a brand new building, patterning it after one of ours. After he had been in the bird business for several years, he told me that he could make more money off of a good pair of parakeets per year than he could off of a mother cow. I asked him how he arrived at that conclusion. He explained that by the time he figured the cost of the land, the cattle, the fencing, corrals, barns, tractors, trailers, hay baling equipment and veterinary costs, he could end up with more net profit per year with a good pair of parakeet breeders than he could with a mother cow. Dr. Barron said that he could clear more money per year with less effort on 100 pair of good parakeet breeders than he could with 100 head of mother cows. I guess he should have known, he raised them both. In addition, Dr. Barron pointed out that with the birds he didn't have to get out in the winter weather with them like he did with his cows. I have had others to share similar stories with me through the years. When I was first investigating the bird business back in the early 70's, an old retired rancher who was then raising parakeets told me almost the exact same thing and his advice was instrumental in my decision to enter the business.

Hopefully these figures will give you an idea of what a person can expect to make raising birds. There is some very good money to be made raising these different types of birds if you do it properly. It is, of course, a numbers game. The more birds you produce, the more you can make. Also, this business is just like any other in that you will have people come and go. The ones who like it and manage their business properly, will almost always grow. The ones who don't, quit. Some of the more successful breeders will grow to have several thousand pair of breeding birds. It can be a great part-time business if you just want some extra spending money, or it can be a very good living. The opportunity is there, its all up to you.

Chapter 4
Different Ways In Which To Market Your Birds

Breeding birds is not really that hard to do at all, and as you can see from the preceding chapter, it can be quite profitable. At the beginning of this book we clearly show that there is a strong demand for pet birds in this country. Although the demand is there, you will still need to choose some means by which to market them. The way in which you go about marketing your birds will determine how much money you make breeding your birds and how much enjoyment you get out of the whole business. You may enjoy the breeding part of the business and dislike the marketing part. The way you go about selling your birds will be determined by how many breeding pairs you have and how much time you are willing to devote to selling them.

The Bird Buyer

By far the easiest and simplest way to sell your birds is to sell them to a bird buyer who is a wholesale distributor. This is a person who buys birds from you and wholesales them to pet shops and other distributors. Bird buyers usually move large volumes of birds. You will find in this business that a good, honest, reputable and reliable buyer is worth his or her weight in gold. You may be very, very good at raising birds, but lack the time, desire, or skills necessary to sell your birds profitably in the marketplace. A good buyer will allow you to spend much more time with your breeding operation and less time marketing birds.

Most bird buyers have quite a few breeders that they regularly buy from. While some buyers will come to your place and pick the birds up, others will have a location that you will deliver the birds to. You should be very cautious and careful when allowing a buyer to

The greatest backyard business ever!

what are the precautions?

pick up birds at your place. Buyers handle birds from all over the country and can be a good source to bring a disease into your flock if you don't take the necessary precautions.

As a general rule, buyers will prefer to buy your birds every two to four weeks, since baby birds are what they have the biggest demand for. A good buyer must also pay fair market prices throughout the year.

Although a good buyer is worth a lot, it's a two way street. As a breeder, in order for you to depend on him, he must be able to depend on you. When he needs birds and you have them to sell, then by all means let him, your regular buyer, buy them. He has regular customers who depend on him for their supply of birds, and he depends on breeders like you for his supply. There will be times when the demand for birds far exceeds the available supply, such as a few weeks before Mothers Day, Valentines Day, Christmas, etc. After you have been in the business for a while and become known as a quality breeder, when the demand is strong for birds you will no doubt get calls from other buyers offering to pay you a little more for your birds than your regular buyer is paying. It happens all the time. But as soon as the demand and the supply begin to level off, the buyer offering above market price will usually disappear. Unless your regular buyer is unable to handle all of your birds and the two of you have discussed it, don't fall for that trick. After all, you wouldn't like it if someone offered your regular buyer birds a little under market price and he didn't take your birds because he could temporarily get them a little cheaper elsewhere. Always remember that your buyer is depending on you just as much as you are depending on him. I usually considered buyers who would jump in and offer a quarter a bird more when the demand was the greatest, and then disappear when the peak demand was over, to be unethical and better left alone. However, if there are many birds in your area, there very well can be several buyers to choose from, and depending on your size, you may elect to sell to more than one buyer.

After you have been breeding birds for a while you will be able to distinguish a cull bird from a good one, as well as a sickly bird from a healthy one. Some buyers have found a market for cull birds, but there is NO market for sickly birds. Absolutely, under no circumstances, should a breeder ever attempt to sell a sickly bird to the buyer. Although a good buyer will almost always be able to identify the sickly bird while he is grading and counting the birds, sometimes one will slip by. At that point, either he or his customer who he sells the bird to will suffer the loss. Or worse yet, some little child could buy it from the retail pet shop and take it home, only to have it die, at which time the youngster is heartbroken and may never buy another bird again.

Once you have been in the business for a while you will most likely come to know who is buying birds in the area within a hundred miles or so of where you live. But when you are first starting out in the business, you may have to locate a buyer. Check with the local feed stores in your area and see which ones are selling bird feed. Ask them if they know if there is a buyer in the area. If they can't put you in contact with a buyer, then ask them who is breeding birds in the area and go to those people to see if they are selling to a buyer. A feed store should be helpful, since they make their living selling feed and supplies. Many feed stores will even provide a place for a buyer to come and buy birds from the local breeders. That gives them an edge over other feed stores in that the breeders will usually buy all their supplies where they sell their birds. It's a matter of convenience if they can do that. I once set up a buying station at Marshall Grain Company, a large feed store in Fort Worth, Texas. After I had been buying there five or six years the manager told me that their bird feed business had more than doubled since I had started buying. No question about it, a buyer will attract customers to a feed store.

In the event the area you live in has no buyer, you may have to drive to another area to market your birds. In the beginning I drove from my hometown of Corsicana, Texas to Waco, which was about 50 miles, to sell my birds. If there is not a bird buyer in your given area,

The greatest backyard business ever! 49

as more birds become available in that area, rest assured that a buyer will start coming when the supply exist.

Selling your birds to a buyer is certainly not the only way to market them, but it is overall, by far the easiest way. Just remember to choose a buyer who is honest, reliable, ethical and knows the meaning of the word "integrity". If there is not a buyer in your area that fits that description, then you might want to consider becoming one. The income potential is huge. We'll cover that option a little later in the book.

Selling Directly to Pet Shops

Although selling birds directly to pet shops will usually bring you more money for your birds, it is much more time consuming. The decision as to whether to sell to a buyer, a pet shop, or a group of shops should be based on the amount of time you are willing to spend selling your birds, as well as the size of your breeding operation and your location. If you are a rather small breeder, you will probably not be able to ship your birds nationwide as small shipments are usually cost prohibitive. Live animal airfreight rates are costly, usually running anywhere from 150% to 250% of the cost of regular freight. You might think, yeah, but birds don't weigh much. That's right, but they take up quite a bit of space. Airlines have figured that out so they charge you by dimensional weight if the box is too light.

Bear in mind, in order to sell to pet shops you certainly don't always have to ship your birds. It would just depend on where you live. Obviously, if you live in a large city there will be a number of pet shops that are potential customers. Selling directly to pet shops in a small town will, of course, limit the volume of birds that you could expect to move because of the smaller number of shops to sell to. Birds that you sell directly to the pet shops, depending on the type of bird it is, will usually bring anywhere from 25% to 40% more than what you could expect to receive from a bird buyer, but again, it's usually more time consuming.

Bird Marts, Pet Expos and Bird Fairs

These go by different names in different areas, but basically they are the same thing and are very similar to a trade show, if you have ever been to one of those. There are companies that promote and put these events on throughout the country. The most recent one that I attended was in San Antonio, Texas, and I was really impressed with the turnout of people that were there. I could hardly find a place to park. There were probably close to 150 vendors inside the huge exhibit hall who had booths set up selling just about every imaginable kind of bird and bird related products. The event had been well advertised and was held at a very large civic center and was open to the public. I simply couldn't believe how many people that were there. People came there from all over the country, both buying and selling birds and bird products. I talked to one vendor who was there all the way from California. He was selling a variety of birds and said that he came to that particular show every time, and it is held several times a year. He obviously must have been doing pretty well in order to justify coming back all that distance several times a year.

The birds at these shows bring much higher prices than you will get from either a buyer or a pet shop. They pretty much bring close to retail prices, some even above retail, as there will usually be quite a few hand fed babies there, including hand fed baby parakeets and cockatiels. Those handfed babies always bring big bucks.

These shows are held from coast to coast and border to border and constitute just one more way in which to market your birds. Some breeders attend several of these on a regular basis and move the majority of their birds this way. The drawback is that they require a considerable amount of time and are not usually a way in which you could move a really large volume of birds, although they do bring much higher prices. You can usually find a list of the locations where

The greatest backyard business ever!

these shows are being held, along with the dates and phone numbers in cage bird or other pet trade magazines.

The Overlooked Markets

Trade days, open air markets, street markets, peddler's fairs, swap meets or flea markets. They go by different names in different parts of the country, but they are all about the same. They are yet another method in which you can market your birds that is often overlooked. Like the bird marts and expos previously discussed, this is not a way in which you can move a really huge volume of birds, but I do know of people who do quite well selling birds through these types of markets. Because their overhead is less than other retail outlets, people who choose to sell at flea markets (that's what I call them) will usually sell their birds below retail price, but for more than they would receive from a wholesale buyer. In addition to birds, most people who sell at flea markets will also sell bird cages and supplies. Cages and supplies have a very good mark up, which adds to your bottom line. Some of the people who sell at these trade days or flea markets have been doing it for many years, which would seem to indicate that they are turning a fair profit. I know a couple of people who sell monthly at flea markets, and although they are not huge breeders, they cannot produce enough birds themselves and are forced to buy from other breeders to meet their flea market demand. I personally know of one man who has been doing this very successfully for over 20 years.

I used to think that flea markets were made up of nothing but junk dealers. Although a lot of them are just that, it's certainly not the case with all of them. Some flea markets handle quality stuff, and lots of it. Advertised as the largest one in the world, Canton, Texas has a three-day flea market held once a month, 12 months out of the year. To give you an idea of its size, it has over 100 acres of parking, and usually around 5,000 vendors.... people selling every imaginable thing. I have never seen anything like it. They advertise an average attendance of between 100,000 to 300,000 during that 3-

day event each month, sometimes even having close to a million shoppers in the prime months. That's a lot of people for a 3 day market. They have 20 acres devoted to the selling of animals and animal related products...just about every imaginable type of domesticated animal is sold there.

There are a number of these types of markets located all around the country that are almost as big, some maybe even bigger, even though Canton claims to be the biggest. Bookstores sell flea market directories that list these markets on a state by state basis, including the statistics that go with them. There is no question about it, trade days, flea markets, or what ever you want to call them, are a way in which many people market their birds on a regular basis at near retail prices. But it is time consuming, and not a way in which you can move thousands of birds on a monthly basis, but for those who enjoy this type of event and do not need to move thousands of birds monthly, the opportunity is surely there.

Retail

Lastly, if you are a small breeder located on a busy, well traveled road, a nice sign properly placed can often allow you to move most of your offspring at retail prices. I know of bird breeders who have marketed their birds for many, many years in just this manner, and they have done well. I have also known people to set up a roadside shop on weekends selling birds as well as cages and supplies, very similar to what many people do with vegetable and fruit stands. Apparently they do reasonably well, since many of those same people will be there year after year. Other breeders will market their birds through newspaper advertising, or a combination of these different ways. Since I always worked on volume, I have never marketed birds in a retail manner, but there are others who have done it year after year. They like it and have done very well.

In conclusion, the size of your breeding operation will determine the volume of birds you will need to move. The amount of time you are willing to devote to moving that volume will determine the method that best meets your needs. For the larger commercial breeders, by far the easiest and simplest method in which to market your birds is through a reputable buyer who is a nationwide wholesale distributor. That will allow you to devote much more time to your breeding operation.

Part II

Chapter 5
Becoming A Wholesale Distributor Of Pet Birds

Check out Cage Bird Magazines.

At the beginning of this book I mentioned why we got into the wholesale/distributing part of the bird business. The demand was there and we just could not produce enough birds for our customers. However, we got into it out of necessity and not by choice. Looking back, I believe that it was one of the best things that could have happened to us. There is no question about it, a wholesale distributor of pet birds can make money, and I'm talking about A LOT OF MONEY. It's a volume business, plain and simple. The more birds you move, the more money you will make. A good wholesale distributor can make from $50,000 to $200,000 a year, even as a mom and pop operation. I personally know of some that have become very wealthy in this part of the bird business. I also know a few that have failed miserably.

The ones that failed, was it because of no demand for birds? I hardly think so. Venture department stores, Montgomery Wards, Ben Franklin stores, K-Mart, all have declared bankruptcy. After 117 years in business, the F.W. Woolworth company closed its doors. Were all of these because of lack of demand, while at the same time, Wal-Mart, which carries basically the same products, has grown into the world's largest retailer? Of course not. The eminent success or failure of almost any business lies in the decisions of management and their ability to constantly make changes when changes are needed. The absolute same is true in the bird business. While some wholesale distributors make good decisions, remain honest, practice good business ethics and take good care of their customers, others don't. Some allow greed to take over, often taking advantage of the very people who are keeping them in business. That may last for a short

The greatest backyard business ever!

time, but usually not for long. Greed has led to the downfall of more than one wholesale distributor. But for the person who is willing to work hard at it, this part of the bird business offers an almost unlimited opportunity. I hasten to add that this business does not discriminate on the basis of sex. I have known both men and women who were successful as wholesale distributors of birds.

At this point I think I should maybe back up and fill in a few blanks about how we came about from being strictly a parakeet breeder to a breeder/wholesale distributor. It could very well help you if you decide to get into this part of the business. At the very least, it should give you encouragement if times get tough.

When we entered the bird business, I clearly had done my homework and had determined that the demand was there, so we started out with the parakeets in a small building in our backyard in 1975. By 1976 we had sold quite a few birds and they were bringing what we thought to be very good prices. The buyer was paying us between $5 and $5.50 each and he was always wanting more. As a breeder, you can make a LOT of money at those prices. Based on that, we expanded by building 6 more small 12 x 16 ft. buildings in the pasture next to our house. Being a young couple, we didn't have a lot of money and had sunk most of our savings in those little buildings and the birds inside them. Fortunately for us, those six little buildings just turned into birds. Maybe beginners luck, I don't know, but I think that their production was as good as any birds that I have ever had. Anyway, I figured we were headed towards easy street and that the bank would soon be building a branch office out our way to help handle things.

Although I had carried birds to Waco in the beginning and sold to a buyer there, we now had a buyer who came to Corsicana every two weeks to pick up birds in our area. I was young and inexperienced, and I didn't know anything about choosing a reputable buyer; all I knew was that they were wanting birds and were paying big bucks for them, and I had those six little buildings that were coming into full production and dollar signs were in my eyes.

The evening before the buyer would come the next day, I would catch up the birds that were ready to sell and keep them in the carrying cages overnight, as I didn't have time the next morning, since I was still working on the potato chip route.

I will NEVER forget, we had just caught up our biggest crop of birds yet, if memory serves me right, somewhere around 500, which would have brought us over $2500, and that was a lot of money back in 1976 for a young couple, when the buyer calls up and said that the bottom had fell out of the bird market and he didn't know when or if he would ever be back. He then hung up the phone. Talk about letting the air out of your bubble or the lead falling out of your pencil, I'm here to tell you that I don't think I had ever been more depressed or down on things than I was right after that phone call. In my mind, that phone call turned my easy street into skid row. By now my wife was expecting our first child and hopes of a stay at home mom were looking slim. We were about broke as we had sunk almost everything we had into the bird business and had really counted on selling those birds. A call the next morning to the buyer in Waco wasn't much better. Although they didn't say the bottom had fell out of the market, they were not buying all of everybody's birds. They would only buy half of what you brought, and the price was down.

At that point I had a decision to make. You may someday have to make the same decision if your market stalls. I could have either chose to sit back and do nothing and hope things would get better, open the doors and let the birds out and forget the whole thing, or decide to do something about it. Although I didn't know exactly what was going on with the market right then, I felt that I had done my homework and that there truly was a market for these birds. I chose to do something about it. Opportunity can be and often is disguised as adversity, and that proved to be the case in this situation.

With a pregnant wife and about broke, I desperately needed to sell those birds. Remember, my birds were just coming into full production and I had been expecting to sell several hundred of them every couple of weeks. Well, as it turned out, I was able to sell about

The greatest backyard business ever! 59

half of them to the buyer in Waco on a regular basis, although the price did drop considerably.

Sometime back I had noticed a small ad in a cage bird magazine that simply read "birds wanted" and gave a phone number. I dug the ad out and called the number and it was a small chain of pet shops in the Cincinnati, Ohio area. I believe they had 5 locations at the time. They told me what price they were paying and I don't remember just what it was, but I do remember that it was the most that I had ever received for parakeets. I couldn't exactly figure it out. Back home my regular buyer wasn't buying at all, and the other buyer had us on a quota, yet this outfit was willing to pay me more than I had ever received for a bird, and they wanted them on a regular basis. One problem. I had never shipped a bird and didn't have a clue as to what to do. The problem was solved by the manager of one of the stores as he told me exactly what to do and how to do it. I could tell that he wanted my birds and I sure wanted him to have them. To make a long story short, I made my first shipping crates out of potato chip boxes with screen wire stapled in the sides so that the birds could get air. I took them to Dallas/Ft. Worth airport, put them on a plane to Cincinnati, and the manager was true to his word and sent me a check for the birds within a week.

That was my first experience shipping birds. Soon afterwards the local buyers began to take all the birds they could get again. Although I sold to them, I continued to ship birds to that chain of pet shops on a regular basis. I am proud to say that when we sold our business a few years ago, they were still one of our regular customers. Through the years our business relationship grew, and they even referred other pet shops to us from time to time.

I know its an old cliche, but how many times have we heard it- when life gives you a lemon, make lemonade. That buyer calling up and telling me that the bottom had fell completely out of the bird market and that he didn't know when or if he would ever be back, proved to be the lemon that made our lemonade. Had he continued to have been a steady reliable buyer, I might have never gotten into the wholesale/distributor end of the bird business. I don't even remember why he quit buying for the short time that he did, but I'm sure glad he did, because it gave me a taste of what it was like to ship my own birds and get paid premium prices for them. This business is not unlike others in that it experiences temporary seasonal slowdowns and that was probably the case at that time, I don't know. Whatever the case, it was short-lived and it gave me a golden opportunity to get started as a buyer.

By 1978 I had landed several other nationwide accounts and we could not keep up with the demand out of our own production and I was forced to start buying birds from other breeders to ship with our own. That year I was able to quit the potato chip route and from then on we were in the bird business on a full-time basis, both as a breeder and a wholesale distributor. Although mine has been a success story, I tell it not in a bragging way. The opportunities were there and the Good Lord allowed me to recognize and capitalize on them. Sometimes you just have to open your eyes and look around a bit to recognize those things. Opportunities are still very much alive today in this business for those who are willing to seek them out.

I'm not telling this story to impress you, but to show you how really simple it was. I believe that if I was able to succeed in this business, that practically anyone can. Sure, you will have to make some logical business decisions, but besides that, all it really takes is some determination and dedication on your part. Some motivation- being almost broke with an expectant wife gave me the motivation I needed. Some enthusiasm-shipping my own birds and receiving the highest price I had ever gotten gave me the enthusiasm I needed. Educate yourself on what is going on in the business. Do your homework well and don't believe everything you hear. Use common sense, be positive and believe in yourself. If others have done it, you can do it too.

Now that you know the reason why we got into the wholesale/distributor part of this business, I'll now show you how we went about building it into a very profitable full time business and how you can do the same. It didn't happen overnight, but year after year we did experience strong growth, until the late 1980's at which time we decided that we were as big as we wanted to be and we simply quit trying to grow. We decided we did not want the headache that comes with having a lot of employees but instead wanted to remain more or less a family run business. The way we built our business doesn't represent the only way in which it can be done, but it certainly worked well for us. By following our methods as well as incorporating ideas of your own, you should be able to achieve success as you become a wholesale distributor of pet birds. It is a wonderful occupation!

Chapter 6
How To Build Your Markets And Your Customer Base

Pet Bird Magazines

There are a number of methods that you can utilize to build your customer base and we will go over what I consider to be the most effective. If you will recall, earlier I mentioned that my first sales lead from an out of state customer came from a "want ad" that had been run in a bird magazine. As I am writing this, I picked up the latest copies of *Bird Talk* and *The A.F.A. Watchbird*. Both magazines have "birds wanted" ads in them. One of the ads reads as follows… "Attention Pet Bird Breeders, wholesaler of high national distribution looking to develop ongoing business," and the ad goes on to list a variety of birds wanted. Obviously this is not a pet shop but a wholesaler who sells to pet shops. Many of these wholesalers are regional wholesalers that are located in a large metropolitan areas. They will operate out of centrally located warehouse and have delivery trucks that deliver birds, and in many cases small animals, reptiles and tropical fish to the retail stores in their area. Some of these wholesale distributors use huge volumes of birds. In my case, even though I was a wholesale distributor, I was located in a somewhat rural area of Texas, and had no local market that I desired to cultivate. I was located 50 miles from the Dallas/Ft.Worth metroplex, which is the 9th largest metropolitan area in the nation. There was ample opportunity for me to work that market if I chose to, but I did not like the idea of delivering to the many different areas of the metroplex. I am a country boy at heart, and I just didn't care for the traffic and hassle of the big city. I would rather deliver all of my birds to the airport and ship them, letting the airport be my one and only delivery point. But there are others who don't mind the traffic, and these people are usually rewarded handsomely for their efforts.

As you build your business you will probably want to sell to pet shops as well as to other distributors such as the one mentioned in the ad. But I have known some buyers who sold exclusively to other wholesalers only, choosing not to sell to the individual pet shops. That can certainly work well, and can be a lot less trouble. You will have to give the wholesale distributors a good price break in order to get and keep their business, but they usually move large volumes of birds, and again, its much less trouble.

You might wonder why a wholesale distributor might run an ad such as the one mentioned above and why you as a buyer or wholesale distributor might want to sell to him. He ran the ad because he can't get enough birds in his local area. However, you might be in an area where a good pocket of breeders exists, and you could simply buy from them and ship to him. Its crazy, but he might turn around and ship a load of birds to a pet shop or group of shops that are within 10 miles of the very airport that you shipped your birds to him from. That happens all the time. I used to ship large amounts of parakeets to a wholesale distributor in Florida. Sometimes when I would be at the Dallas airport shipping birds to him in Florida, I would see parakeets that he had just shipped in from Florida. Some of the birds could have easily been birds that I had shipped to him the week before from Texas, and now, here they were back in Dallas. He was a full line livestock wholesaler, offering a complete line of birds, fish and small animals, and for convenience, some pet shops will only buy from the full line wholesale distributors.

Another important thing worth mentioning. If I were selling to a wholesale distributor in, lets say Chicago, then I would not solicit business from any of the pet shops in that area if that distributor was a regular customer of mine. That's just good business. Don't try to compete for business with a wholesale distributor whom you are supplying birds to in an area where they are located. If you get calls from potential customers in that area, refer them to the distributor that you supply in their area.

In regards to the earlier mentioned "bird wanted ad", if I were selling all the birds that I had and not in need of any new customers, then I would clip and save the ad for future use. I might even call and find out a little more about their needs and give them my number for their files. Other dealers will keep a list of phone numbers that they will use when they are having trouble getting enough birds for whatever the reason might be, so make sure they have your number in their files.

Of course, in addition to the want ads in the bird magazines, you can run your own ads offering birds for sale. Through the years we were in business, I believe we only ran an ad in a couple of magazines for a month or so. We just never really needed to. I cannot stress it enough, when you land a new customer, treat them fairly and only sell healthy birds of the finest quality and you will have them as repeat customers for a long, long time. You will be surprised, but it just doesn't take a large amount of customers to buy a lot of birds, if they are regular, repeat buyers. A handful of good customers can sometimes be all you need. While pet bird magazines are geared mainly to the hobbyist and not the commercial producer, nevertheless, they can be an avenue in which you can make contacts. There are a number of these magazines on the market, several of which are listed below.

Bird Talk Magazine
P.O. Box 57347
Boulder, CO 80322-7347
Phone 800-365-4421
Fax 641-842-6101

Bird Times
7-L Dundas Circle
Greensboro, NC 27407
Phone 336-292-4047
Fax 336-292-4272

The greatest backyard business ever!

A.F.A. Watchbird Magazine
American Federation of Aviculture
P.O. Box 56218
Phoenix, AZ 85079-6218
Phone 602-484-0931
Fax 602-484-0109

Pet Trade Publications

These are monthly publications with large circulations that go mostly to industry professionals such as retail pet outlets, feed dealers, pet supply wholesalers, livestock wholesalers and others in the pet industry. These trade magazines can be a very effective way of reaching and developing your market. Qualified members of the pet industry can get free subscriptions to these trade magazines, and as a wholesale distributor of birds, you will be qualified. In addition to the monthly magazines, most of these publications will produce "directories" or "buyer's guides". Some of these "buyer's guides" are published annually, some semi-annually. These big directories are like the "yellow pages" of the pet industry. They have thousands of companies broken down into various categories according to what products or livestock they supply. As a wholesale distributor of birds, you will be entitled to a free listing in these directories. Since these have a large circulation, they are the best method I know of to get your name into the hands of potential buyers at no cost to you. For even more exposure, especially when starting out, it's not a bad idea to purchase a display ad in one or more of these directories.

When we were first starting out and were building our customer base, if we needed to move additional birds, I would take one of these directories and turn to the livestock section and see what wholesalers were listed under the type of birds that we were needing to move. I'd give them a call, and if they were not interested at the time, I would find out all I could about them and make notes for future reference, and then call the next one on the list. I have moved tens of thousands of extra birds in this way, all the time building a larger customer base. It was through those directories that I landed some of my largest volume customers. These directories were, and continue to be a very valuable source of information for acquiring new customers, and best of all, as a wholesale distributor, the subscriptions and a basic listing are free.

There are currently 3 of these publications.

Pet Product News
P.O. Box 16509
North Hollywood, CA 91615
Phone 818-760-8904
Fax 818-760-4490
Magazine published monthly
Directory published semi-annually

Pet Business
233 Park Ave. South
6th Floor
New York, NY 10003
Phone 212-979-4828
Fax 212-228-3142
Magazine published monthly
Directory published semi-annually

Pet Age
H.H. Backer Associates, Inc.
200 S. Michigan Ave.
Suite 840
Chicago, IL 60604
Phone 312-663-4040
Fax 312-663-5676
Magazine published monthly
Directory published annually

Great for Getting your business in the customers eye.

Good Place to List your business & What you have for Sale.

These publications have a circulation of between 23,000 and 25,000 each and are targeted towards key decision makers and business owners, so you can see that to be listed in these directories will put your name in front of a lot of the right people. Don't pass it up, it's free.

Trade Shows

There are about a half dozen very large pet industry trade shows that are held annually or semi-annually across the United States. Some of these shows are huge with as many as 1,000 booths that will be occupied by some 600 to 700 exhibitors. These shows will usually last around 3 days and will attract thousands of potential buyers and contacts. These shows are not open to the public, therefore the people who attend these are the BUYERS from the companies they represent. Most of the exhibitors will be companies that are either manufacturers or distributors of almost anything pertaining to the pet industry. There are usually very few actual livestock vendors who will have a booth at these shows. If you are in need of new business, these shows can be a great way to get your name in the eyes of the retailers and wholesalers who attend these trade shows.

Even if you are not an exhibitor, you can benefit from these events. Although the shows are not open to the public, qualified individuals with the proper credentials are admitted free of charge. If you are a legitimate wholesale distributor you will be qualified, although you would need to contact whoever is sponsoring the show to see what credentials are needed for admittance. Once inside, remember that most of the people attending these shows are either owners or representatives of companies that have come to the show looking to see new products and to meet new vendors. You would be hard pressed to find a better place that has a higher concentration of the very people that you will be doing business with. Many of these people can be your future customers.

Make sure you have an ample supply of business cards to hand out as you mingle and talk to the show attendees. Selling birds is a little bit like selling real estate in some ways, but a whole lot better in other ways. You might hand out several hundred business cards before you hand one to the right person and make a sale. In real estate, when you make the sale that's it, its over. You collect your commission and go on passing out more cards looking for the next sale. In this business, once you have made the sale, if you handle quality stock and treat the customer fairly, you can expect to continue to sell to that same customer over and over on a weekly, semi-weekly or monthly basis for years to come. What ever you do, develop a good relationship with your customers so that you can continue to supply them in the years ahead, and as they expand and grow their own businesses, as their supplier, your business will grow automatically. Always remember these two points, it just doesn't take a lot of decent size customers to keep a wholesale distributor in business, and these trade shows attract the heavy weights in the industry. The trade magazines mentioned earlier usually will have these show dates and times listed as well as contact information. Some of the *"buyers guides"* will also have a yearly calendar of events that includes this information. Although these trade shows are national in scope, to a degree they could be considered somewhat heavier weighted in regional attendance. For instance, if I were targeting the northeastern part of the country as my main market area, I would probably shoot for attending one of the trade shows that was being held in that area over one that was being held in another part of the country.

Business Lists

With over 12 million businesses in the United States, there are companies that specialize in compiling enormous databases of information that can provide you with sales leads and mailing lists related to just about every imaginable type of business. These lists are compiled from phone books and yellow page ads as well as many other sources. The bottom line is, if the business has a phone with a

The greatest backyard business ever!

listed number, it will probably be included in these business list databases.

There are currently over 8,000 retail pet shops in the United States that make up your targeted market as a wholesale distributor. You can purchase a list of retail pet shop names from these companies for as little as 8 cents each. These list include basic information such as company name and address, and for a penny or so more you can get the phone number included. Of course it comes at an increased cost, but you can get even more detailed information such as the name and title of key executives, number of employees, estimated annual sales volume, year the business was established, even the square footage of the business. You can purchase these list on printed labels, paper or cd, depending on what's included on the list. One of the good things about these list is that you do not have to buy the whole thing. They are broken down on a state by state basis, which really makes it nice if you are just targeting certain areas of the country. I believe we only bought the list twice, and not the whole thing then. Just our targeted market. The first time we bought the list, I ordered the adhesive labels to put on a mail-out of fliers that we had printed up and the results were not as good as we had hoped for. The next time I ordered the paper print out of the selected states we were targeting, and paid the few additional cents to included the phone numbers. That proved to get much better results.

In order for mail-outs to be effective, they need to be done a number of times. Although you can get bulk rates, postage is still expensive, but if you purchase the list that includes the fax numbers, you can fax monthly flyers to select businesses instead of mailing them. With all the inexpensive long distance phone plans available now, in my opinion, sending flyers by fax or making telephone sales calls can be the most effective way to build your business.

You will probably want to target specific states as you build your nationwide business. There are a number of different reasons for this, not the least being the airline service of the airport you plan on shipping from. We shipped our birds out of Dallas/Ft.Worth

70 *Raising Pet Birds For Profit*

International airport, which is the third busiest in the nation. It was serviced by virtually every major airline, so shipping destinations were never a major factor with us. However, some of the smaller airports are only serviced by one or two major airlines. That can have a negative impact on your ability to ship to the various places you might want to ship your birds to.

Live animal freight is much different than passenger travel. As high as freight rates already are, they skyrocket even more and usually become cost prohibitive if the shipment has to change airlines. While changing planes within the same airline is alright, changing airlines with a shipment of birds is an entirely different matter. Airlines have minimum freight rates and your customer will be charged at least the minimum rate by both airlines if you have to connect your shipment with another airline. And believe me, your customer won't be a happy camper about that. Try to avoid it if at all possible. It would be much better for you to target areas of the country that the major airlines servicing your airport fly into.

Another reason you will want to target specific states for your business is because of the health rules and regulations required for interstate shipments of birds by each specific state. Some states have almost none, while others have so many regulations that they simply aren't worth the trouble. For instance, some states require certain birds to be banded. For years, the state of California required parakeets being shipped into the state to be banded with a numbered, dated, closed ring legband. Banding birds with closed ring legbands is a lot of trouble, not to mention the cost. Therefore, we chose not to ship parakeets into the state of California. Because of that law, parakeets sold for more money in California than in most other places, but it just wasn't worth the hassle. That law has since been repealed, which has opened up a whole new market for those living outside of the state of California.

Some states will require different types of permits, but these are usually free of charge and no trouble to get. Some will require health certificates to accompany the shipment, which must be issued

The greatest backyard business ever!

by a veterinary in the state of origin. These will usually cost from $10 to $25 each, but the cost is usually passed on to the customer you are shipping the birds to. These are just a few of the things that you will want to keep in mind as you target your market, although most of these state requirements are not that difficult to comply with.

Rank	Name of Metropolitan Area	States	Population
1	NewYork, Northern New Jersey-Long Island	New York, New Jersey, Connecticut, Pennsylvania	21.2 million
2	Los Angeles-Riverside-Orange county	California	16.4 million
3	Chicago-Gary-Kenosha	Illinois, Indiana	9.2 million
4	Washington-Baltimore	District of Columbia, Maryland, Virginia, West Virginia	7.6 million
5	San Francisco-Oakland-San Jose	California	7.0 million
6	Philadelphia-Wilmington-Atlantic City	Pennsylvania, New Jersey, Delaware, Maryland	6.2 million
7	Boston-Worchester-Lawrence	Massachusetts, New Hampshire, Maine, Connecticut	5.8 million
8	Detroit-Ann Arbor-Flint	Michigan	5.5 million
9	Dallas-Fort Worth	Texas	5.2 million
10	Houston-Galveston-Brazoria	Texas	4.7 million
11	Atlanta	Georgia	4.1 million
12	Miami-Fort Lauderdale	Florida	3.9 million
13	Seattle-Tacoma-Bremerton	Washington	3.6 million
14	Phoenix-Mesa	Arizona	3.3 million
15	Minneapolis-St. Paul	Minnesota, Wisconsin	3.0 million

I have included a listing of the 15 largest metropolitan areas in the U.S. Over 30 percent of the entire population of the country is located in the top 10 of these metro areas. These areas definitely should be considered if you plan to purchase a list of business names to use when building your customer base.

After you purchase your list, scan through it looking to see if there are several stores in the same city that are listed under the same name. For instance, if you find 5 *Friendly Critter Pet Centers* located in Boston, your first thoughts would be that the same person or company owns them all, and that very well could be the case. It's possible that it could be a franchised chain with multiple owners, but usually if they are all located in a cluster, there is a good chance they will have the same owner. Multiple stores owned by one owner are usually the best, although that's not always the case, since there are some huge, one location, individually owned pet stores out there. I recently read of an 8,000 square foot individually owned pet shop located in Connecticut that is devoted to birds only. A super shop such as this would be a nice one to supply with birds. Sometimes, one large store such as this will sell more birds than a half dozen smaller stores. This is why a more detailed list that includes the number of employees, square footage of the store and years in business can come in handy. After you have screened through the list and checked off the ones you would like to target as your future customers, the next step is to get busy and become a first class salesperson.

Some people have an extremely outgoing personality that makes them a natural born salesman. If you are not such a person, perhaps the shy type, I would suggest that you either go to the library or bookstore and acquire a few books on selling as well as telephone speaking skills and techniques. Some excellent skills can also be gained by reading books on public speaking, and of course self-motivation books are excellent to help build your confidence. Personally, I believe that sales calls are much more effective than mail-outs, and with long distance calling now so inexpensive, its more cost efficient as well. If you purchase the list that includes fax numbers, you can fax flyers to potential customers for a few pennies a month instead of mailing them.

As you begin making your first sales calls, don't make them to the larger stores or chains at first, unless of course, you have a successful background in selling. Use the smaller stores to perfect your salesmanship skills on. Many times the first impression is the one that lasts, so you don't want to call and ask to speak with the owner of a large chain and come across with something like this; "Hello, my name is uh, John, and I uh, have a uh, bird farm and uh, uh, I was, uh, wondering if, uh, you, uh, uh, might be needing, uh, some, uh, uh, uh, birds." The scope of this book was not intended to teach salesmanship, but to show you where the markets are and how to tap into and develop them. Just remember, there is nothing high tech about this business and you don't have to be a slick talking salesman of the year at a used car dealership in order to succeed in this business. Not at all. But you WILL have to make some sales calls in the beginning, and unless you have a background in selling, you will need to acquire and polish these skills.

By building your business on honesty and integrity and handling quality stock at fair prices, pretty soon your birds should be selling themselves. The last five years or so before we sold our business, I don't think that I made any new sales calls soliciting new customers. We would usually be sold out a week or two in advance by orders from our regular customers. I cannot over emphasize the importance of treating your customers fairly in order to retain their repeat business. You may be surprised, but it just doesn't take very many good customers that buy on a regular basis to consume a lot of birds. Repeat customers will make your life a lot easier and can make you a very good living. Burn that into your mind.

When you are first starting out in business and nobody knows about you, you will have to make your presence known, but as time goes on, you will be surprised at the calls you will get from businesses you have never heard of. I have no idea how many calls we got from people who had copied our phone number off of our shipping boxes at the airport, but it was quite a few. For instance, someone might be picking up a shipment of dogs, fish or birds at the airport and they could see a shipment of your birds sitting on the dock that had just come in. If you've got good looking stock, believe me, they will take notice and will probably write your name and number down for future reference.

I believe these business listings are one of the most cost effective and efficient means of building your business in the beginning. Although I have listed only three of them, there are a number of companies who specialize in these business databases and I would suggest that you compare prices from several of them.

InfoUSA.com
5711 South 86th Circle
Omaha, Neb. 68127
Phone 1-800-321-0869
Fax 1-402-537-6975

Accurate Leads
2920 Horizon Park Dr.
Suite A
Suwanee, Ga. 30024
Phone 1-800-685-4787
Fax 1-678-727-9678

The D & B Corporation
103 JFK Parkway
Short Hills, N.J. 07078
Phone 1-800-234-3867

During our 25 years in the exotic bird and animal business, many of our customers that we sold to became more than just customers, they became friends, although I actually only ever met

The greatest backyard business ever! 75

very few of them in person, since I was located in Texas and they were scattered all over the nation. That just goes to reinforce the fact that you can build and operate this type of business from just about anywhere in the country.

Chapter 7

Getting Started Buying Birds; The Need For A Warehouse

I believe that before you consider becoming a wholesale distributor, you would be wise to breed birds for a year or so first. That is by far the best way that I know of for you to learn the proper feeding and handling techniques, as well as the best way for the newcomer to learn a healthy bird from an unhealthy one. I also think that it is important for you to have sold to another buyer before you strike out on your own. By doing so, you will get a feel for how the grading process goes. My advice would also be for you to gradually and slowly ease into this part of the bird business, not biting off more than you can handle at first. Like almost anything else, there is a learning curve that you will go through, and it is far easier and less costly to learn on a small scale.

As you get into the wholesale distributor part of the pet bird business, you've got to remember that it's a little different from the breeder end of the business where you were only dependent upon selling your birds. With this, you will have to work on both sides of the fence. As a buyer, you are dependent upon the breeders to supply you with birds, and as a seller you are dependent upon the retailers or other wholesalers that you ship to. I truly believe that the reason so many small businesses fail is that the owners fail to realize who the real boss is. The owner is not the boss, the customer is. The customer is the one who will determine if the business is still there next year. As a buyer, I always felt that I had to do everything possible to keep my breeders in business, since they were my source of supply. As a seller, I felt that I had to bend over backwards to give my customers the very best quality of birds and service possible, and at a fair price. I never thought of myself as the boss. I always thought of the customer as the boss; and my thoughts were that I had better please the boss or I'd get fired.

How many times have you been waited on by a store clerk, and he or she made you feel like they were doing you a favor by waiting on you, when, in fact, you were doing them a favor by being there? Without the customer, of whom you are one, the business would not exist and the clerk would have no job. If you will realize the importance of your customers before you start this business, and that without them you won't have a business, then your chances of success are greatly enhanced.

In order to become a buyer, you will need a considerable amount of working capital as well as an adequate facility. Although we were pretty much broke when we started, we did have a big crop of birds to sell, and as we sold them we would use that money to buy more birds from others at lower prices and resale at the higher prices. During the first few years, almost everything we made was plowed right back into the business. We built two more large buildings of 24 ft. x 52 ft. for breeding, and one larger one of 24 ft. x 56 ft. for a warehouse in which to hold birds before shipping. Although our growth was rapid, we started out small and grew into this part of the business and that is my recommendation to anyone who wants to become a wholesale distributor of pet birds. Start small, get the feel of it, and then grow.

As a wholesale distributor of birds you will need to carry a good variety of birds. Variety is the main reason why most of the retail outlets that have their birds shipped to them would rather buy from a distributor than from a breeder. Most breeders only breed one or two varieties of birds, whereas a distributor will usually handle a good assortment. And of course some wholesale distributors will add to their variety by also handling small animals and fish in addition to the birds.

Parakeets are the number one seller of all pet birds, and you will need a good color assortment. The pet trade wants mainly baby parakeets of between 6 and 12 weeks of age, but you will also have markets for a limited amount of adult birds and B-grade or cull birds, which are birds with missing feathers, toes, etc., that are otherwise in good health. These different ages and types of birds will all need to be kept in separate cages or flight pens, if at all possible. In addition to parakeets, you will need to carry zebra finches and cockatiels, which both come in an assortment of colors. Then there are the lovebirds, which are broken down into several different species…the peachface, black mask, blue mask, and fisher. These all make up the best selling types of pet birds, but you may also want to carry a larger variety of other finches as well as doves and canaries. At the time of this writing you can still import about a half dozen types of wild caught finches from Puerto Rico, which is not considered a foreign country, but a U.S. territory. The addition of these birds can add a considerable amount to your yearly income.

The above mentioned birds are pretty much what boiled down to be the money makers for us, with the first four being the bread and butter birds. Some wholesalers will also handle the larger hook bills, but we elected not to, since we never could compete with the importers. However, because they are no longer really imported, that has changed somewhat, but the larger birds are slower sellers and most wholesale distributors operate on birds that sell in volume.

As you get into this business you will see that the ideal situation is for you to buy birds one day, fill your orders and ship them all out, either that night or the next morning. Rarely does it happen just like that. That's why you will need ample warehouse space, and the larger you grow the more space you will need. Our warehouse that measured 24 ft. x 56 ft. was almost always adequate for us, and we would sell as many as 80,000 birds a year.

Your warehouse will need to be insulated and climate controlled. Although most birds can take a very wide range of temperature, they do best between about 65 and 85 degrees. Really, the best rule of thumb is that it should be comfortable for you; if you are comfortable, then the birds will be comfortable.

The greatest backyard business ever!

Adequate ventilation is also a must. At times your building may be brimming full of birds and they can put off a considerable amount of dust. If your building doesn't have windows to raise, you may need to add an exhaust fan or two. Poor ventilation can cause respiratory problems with the birds as well as to yourself.

The building also needs to be as mouse proof as possible, since the feed will attract mice. Our warehouse was built specifically for birds, with concrete floors, insulated walls and ceilings and metal siding. Therefore it wasn't a problem keeping rats or mice out. But its not at all necessary to build a specially designed building. I have known a number of wholesalers to operate out of all sorts of buildings. Anything from a rented space in a strip mall, to an old gas station, even portable buildings have all been successfully adapted and used as a warehouse for birds.

When I first started out as a buyer there were not many birds in my immediate area. As our business grew and I began to need more birds, I would travel to other areas, meet with other breeders and let it be known that I was a buyer looking for birds. This is a business in which there are times that a greedy or less than ethical buyer can take advantage of the breeder. For instance, if it is in the dead heat of the summer and business is slow, some buyers will either completely quit buying for a month or so, or offer the breeders a ridiculously low price for their birds, take it or leave it. Well, what's a breeder to do if he is depending on a single buyer and the buyer does something like that? You can't eat the birds, so you either take the offered price or you take nothing at all. That's why it is sometimes a good idea to have more than one buyer in an area.

Greedy buyers normally won't last for long, as someone will eventually come in and take their business, and that's exactly what we were able to do on more than one occasion while building our business. If you find a group of breeders who are selling to a less than ethical buyer, it can be a golden opportunity for you to expand your business much quicker than normally would be the case.

Admittedly, there are times when the bird business will briefly slow down, such as the dead heat of the summer, or right after Christmas, but those times are usually very brief and predictable.

A good buyer must do everything possible to help his or her breeders through any slow periods, and not take advantage of them by paying some ridiculously low price during those times. If necessary, contact the retailers that you supply, and get them to run sales or bird promotions. Cut them a deal. It may be necessary for you to cut your profit margins considerably, but it will be short lived and you will make it up in the long run. Offer them a deal that they can't refuse. I just cannot over emphasis this point; as a buyer, you must keep the production of offspring produced by your breeders moving at all times at all cost. They are depending on you.

Most legitimate buyers will normally pay pretty close to the same price for birds, and once you get into the business, its no secret what everyone is paying. Believe me, the breeders will keep you posted on that. As a general rule, the markup on birds will be somewhere around 40%, but that can and will vary wildly, depending on the supply and demand. When first starting out and getting established as a buyer, I would sometimes buy and sell birds at the same price if I had to, just in order to build my customer base. For instance, I might pay $3.50 for parakeets, run a special promotional sale and sell them at my cost if I could move 300 to 400 of them in the same day to one customer. You must realize that that wasn't something I did very often, as you certainly can't stay in business very long selling birds at your cost, but in the beginning you must do what ever is necessary as long as it is honest, in order to build your customer base.

As you become known as a reliable and honest buyer, before long, breeders from other areas will possibly be calling to see if you would come to their area and set up a buying station, especially if only one buyer is working their area. Many of them will like to sell to more than one buyer, thus assuring them of a steady market. I was able to set up buying stations in several different towns at feed stores who catered to the bird breeders. The feed store would provide a room where I would buy birds from the local breeders every couple of weeks. The breeders would sell me their birds, buy their feed and supplies from the store and be on their way. Actually, it wasn't any trouble at all for the feed store and it gave them a good calling card to get the people to buy feed and supplies from them. I would be there at 8 in the morning and be out of there usually by noon, sometimes having bought from 500 to 1000 birds during that time. At one point we had bird buying routes throughout north Texas as well as Arkansas and Oklahoma. The ideal thing would be to buy the birds and take them directly to the airport and ship, without ever having to take them back home.

We also began to encourage people in our home area to consider raising birds for us. Since the feed stores in our area didn't sell bird feed, I began to sell it to the local breeders who were raising birds for us. In time, the feed business grew to the point that it would add a considerable amount of income to the bottom line of the business. We not only sold feed, but a complete line of bird supplies such as cages, nest boxes, nets, etc; so much so that we had to build a 30ft. x 60 ft. building to handle the feed business.

One thing that I always tried to remember was that I was primarily in the bird business and not the feed business. Some years feed prices might become extremely high because of a drought or flood in the grain belt that had created a shortage of feed. If feed prices were up and the bird prices were not up enough to compensate for the difference, we would often sell feed at pretty close to our cost, in order to help keep the breeder's profit margin up. Again, our main business was buying and selling birds, not feed. If the breeders don't make decent money, they will go out of business and that hurts you, the buyer. As a buyer, you must do everything possible to help your breeders maintain profitability during temporary business slowdowns. They are your lifeline. Without them, you will be out of business. You can make thousands of dollars per year off of each individual breeder. With some of the larger breeders, it is possible for you to make as much as $5,000 to $10,000 per year off of the birds that you buy from them. All of your breeders, large and small alike, are valuable assets and a wise buyer should never forget that fact. You will find that if you feed others, you will eat well yourself!!!

A good buyer will almost always be needing to get more people into raising birds. At times we would have from 50 to 60 people that we were buying from regularly. Breeders will come and go in this business, and there is a constant turnover of people who breed birds. Although many of the larger breeders have been around for many, many years, this business is not unlike other businesses in its turnover rate. People will go out of business for a number of different reasons, regardless of the amount of money they are making. Health reasons, spouse changing jobs, moving, divorce, retirement, and old age are just a few of the reasons why people will quit breeding birds. For these and other reasons, as a buyer you will always need to be looking a year or so ahead and projecting your needs and recruiting more breeders accordingly. As a buyer, if I wanted a $10,000 raise next year, I knew I would have to sell 5000 to 7000 more birds next year than this year, so you constantly must be looking ahead.

Throughout our years in the business, I don't ever remember discouraging but one person from getting into the bird business. I would, however try to show people which birds were in the greatest demand and suggest that they breed those types. I can remember some years when there would be a temporary glut of one particular type of bird or another and I would try to encourage people to diversify into other varieties. Usually the gluts are short lived, sometimes even followed by a shortage of that type of bird for the next few years. The one person that I did discouraged from getting into the business was a very wealthy individual who had an old building that was rat infested and leaked terribly when it rained. The building just wasn't suitable, and his plans were to hire labors to do all the work of tending to the birds.

Although this man knew nothing at all about raising birds, he had put the pencil to the business end of it and was wanting to invest

The greatest backyard business ever!

strictly to make big money, as he planned on a very large operation. If you don't know anything about the business, it would be hard to hire labors and teach them something you didn't know yourself. I didn't think he would succeed because of the way he was planning on doing things and I intentionally discouraged him. This business thrives on success stories, not failures, and I felt he was destined to fail.

As a buyer, you must make every effort to only handle the best quality and healthiest birds available. Let the customers that you ship to be your best form of advertising. After we had been in business for only a few years, we spent NO money at all on advertising. It wasn't necessary. Since most of the customers we shipped to were also growing their businesses, my theory was that repeat business from them as well as referrals was all that we could keep up with. Some of the pet chains we sold to were growing rapidly and they had shared their growth plans with me. One particular chain of pet shops that we sold to grew from 20 to over 60 shops in the years we were in business. Repeat business from customers such as that will keep you in business. Your business will grow automatically as theirs grows. That's why it is so important to handle only healthy birds of the best quality.

Most of the customers we shipped to either bought from us on a weekly, bi-weekly or monthly basis, and yours will probably be the same. In addition to selling to pet shops, if you intend to grow very big, you will want to also build a business selling to other distributors. We sold to some distributors who had standing orders with us, such as 500 parakeets, 100 finches, and 25 cockatiels and 25 lovebirds every two weeks. You will definitely need to give price breaks to the volume customers such as that. The ideal situation was to stay sold out one to two weeks in advance. Most of the time that was the case, although sometimes it wasn't..

Normally, how we would operate would be as follows. We would have a separate group of breeders that we would buy birds from every week. Usually most of the larger breeders would bring birds in every other week, and the smaller ones once a month. We would usually have assigned weeks for different breeders to bring their birds, otherwise you might get 2000 birds one week and 200 the next. We would buy birds on Mondays, fill our orders and try to ship out on Monday night or Tuesday morning. Usually, as we bought the birds from the breeders, we sorted and graded them and put them immediately into our shipping boxes. At times it would be necessary to ship a couple of times a week, although it was our goal to get it all done at one time.

Since you never bought exactly the amount you needed of each type of bird you sold, you had to warehouse or hold a certain amount of birds. Some birds I could not buy locally and had to buy from other wholesalers in other parts of the country. For instance, I could never get enough blue mask or fisher lovebirds in Texas, but there were always plenty of them in California. I knew a couple of reputable wholesale distributors out there and I would order enough blue mask and fisher lovebirds to justify the freight, so that I would have them to fill my orders. Its just not feasible for a pet shop to order a few birds here and a few there, so a good wholesale distributor will handle a full line of the most popular birds. I think you can see why you will need a decent size warehouse.

Our warehouse, as well as most others that I have seen, had a combination of both flight pens and cages in which to hold birds that were not immediately shipped. Birds that you buy and warehouse almost always seem to do better if kept in the same setting as they were in before you bought them. For instance, parakeets that are cage bred seem to do better if warehoused in cages instead of flight pens. Being shuttled around is stressful to them and often times cage bred birds suddenly released into flight pens will not eat or drink properly and you will suffer losses as a result. However, birds that are raised in flight pens and warehoused in cages seem to adjust better. You might be thinking, why not just have all cages in my warehouse instead of both cages and flights? That is possible, but I really liked to use flight pens whenever possible. Normally, the plumage of birds will hold up much better in flight pens than in

The greatest backyard business ever!

cages, especially if the birds are held for any extended period of time. Finches, in particular, are bad about picking their feathers if large numbers of them are held in cages.

As a buyer, you will get to know your breeders well and will know what type of a breeding setup they have, whether cages or colonies. In the event you have to hold their birds for a few days before you get them shipped out, they will hold up better if warehoused like they were raised.

Most of our flight pens measured 8 x 10 feet, which seemed about right. A little smaller is alright, but if they are larger you will have to chase them from one end of the pen to the other when you get ready to catch them. With an 8 x 10 foot flight pen, you can pretty well stand in the middle and using a bird net with a 3 foot long handle, catch them easily. Be sure and have plenty of perches in both your flight pens and holding cages. Perches can be made from ½ inch dowel rods and should be spaced at least 6 inches apart. If a lot of birds are housed in a cage or pen, perches that are too closely spaced will result in tail feathers being picked by the birds setting on the other perches if they are less than 6 inches apart.

Holding cages can be made in a variety of sizes. Most of ours were about 3 x 3 feet x 2 feet tall and constructed with ½ x 1 inch welded wire.

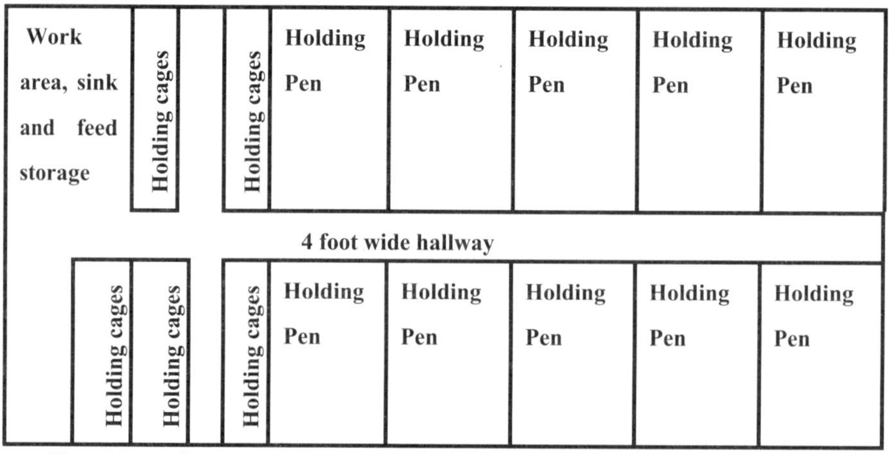
Work area, sink and feed storage
Holding cages
Holding cages
Holding Pen
Holding Pen
Holding Pen
Holding Pen
Holding Pen
4 foot wide hallway
Holding cages
Holding cages
Holding cages
Holding Pen
Holding Pen
Holding Pen
Holding Pen
Holding Pen

Drawing of our warehouse configuration, showing a combination of both holding pens and holding cages.

Your warehouse will need to have a couple of smaller cages set aside to be used as hospital cages. These will need an infrared heat lamp hanging over the perch so that a sickly, injured or stressed bird can get under the lamp as needed. Place a thermometer on the perch and adjust the heat lamp to the correct height so as to get the temperature on the perch to about 85 to 90 degrees, making sure that the entire perch is not covered with the rays of the light, so that the bird can get out of the heat as needed. Often a bird that is stressed and appears sickly can be rejuvenated by simply being kept in a smaller, warm cage for a few days.

Grading and Sorting

When buying birds you will need to grade them closely as to avoid losses, both for you or the customer you are shipping to. Some losses are to be expected and are just part of the business, but buying only healthy birds will help to hold your losses to a minimum. I know that only sounds like a common sense thing, but there are, nevertheless, people who are no longer in this business because they didn't adhere to that very thing. Quality has simply got to be one of your top priorities.

Being able to recognize a healthy bird from a sickly bird is one of the reasons why I think it is so important for anyone to breed birds for a year or so before considering becoming a buyer. You will gain the experience needed and quickly be able to distinguish what's healthy and what's not.

You will need to check for missing toes, check the feathers, eyes, beak and overall health of the bird while you are counting them from the breeders carrying crates into your shipping boxes.

My grading routine would be as follows. Since I am right handed, I would set the breeders carrying cage on a table on my right side and my shipping boxes would be on my left side. I would catch the bird with my right hand and immediately I would get a feel for the bird, whether it is fat, skinny or normal. Buy no skinny or lightweight birds. I would quickly look at both eyes and the beak,

The greatest backyard business ever!

paying close attention to the beak and nostrils to make sure there was no discharge, which would indicate respiratory problems. Holding the birds head between the thumb and index finger so as not to get bitten, I would flip it upside down, looking at its vent for signs of diarrhea, which could indicate an infectious disease, and also checking its feet for deformities or missing toes. Normally a missing toe will not make the bird unsaleable and can be looked over. A point worth mentioning is that if you start noticing a lot of missing toes on a particular breeders birds, the breeder probably has rats in his building. Rats will sometimes chew the toes off of the birds at night if the birds are clinging to the side of the cages or flights as some of them often do.

I'd make sure the birds tail feathers were intact, as well as I'd spread at least one wing looking for missing feathers. You are not looking for a single missing feather, but a group of missing feathers, either primary or secondary feathers. Almost always, if one wing is good or bad the other wing will match. You do not want the tiny pinfeathers to be picked either. If you are not familiar with handling birds, you might think this above procedure would be difficult and time consuming. Not really. If we were strictly grading and sorting, either my wife or myself could count and box for shipping about 500 parakeets or finches in an hour. Cockatiels and lovebirds will take a little longer, but it all goes pretty fast after you get the hang of things. It takes almost as much time labeling the boxes and shuffling the breeders coups around in your buying room than it does counting and grading. As a general rule, most of the time when you first pick the bird up and get the feel of it, you will know if it's a good one or not.

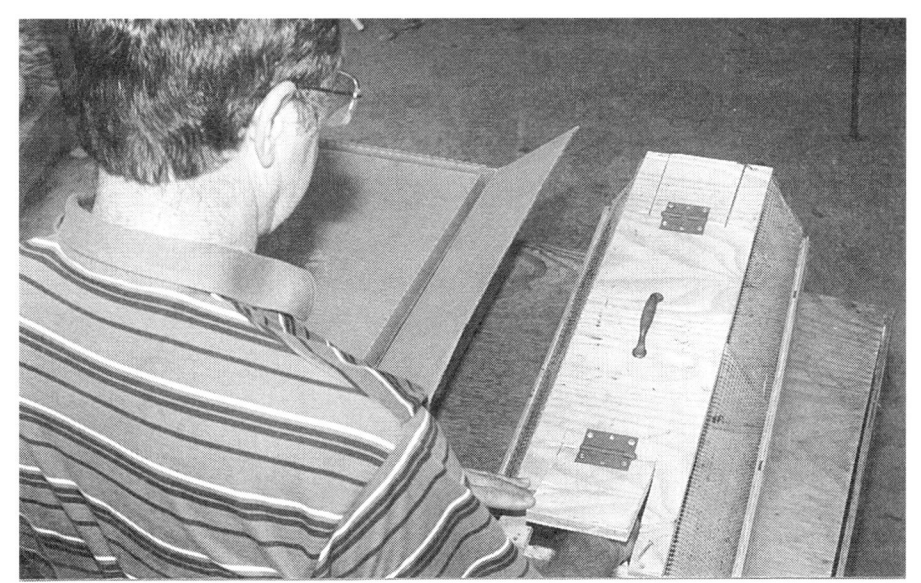

Since I am right handed, I would use the above setup when buying birds. I would catch the bird with my right hand,

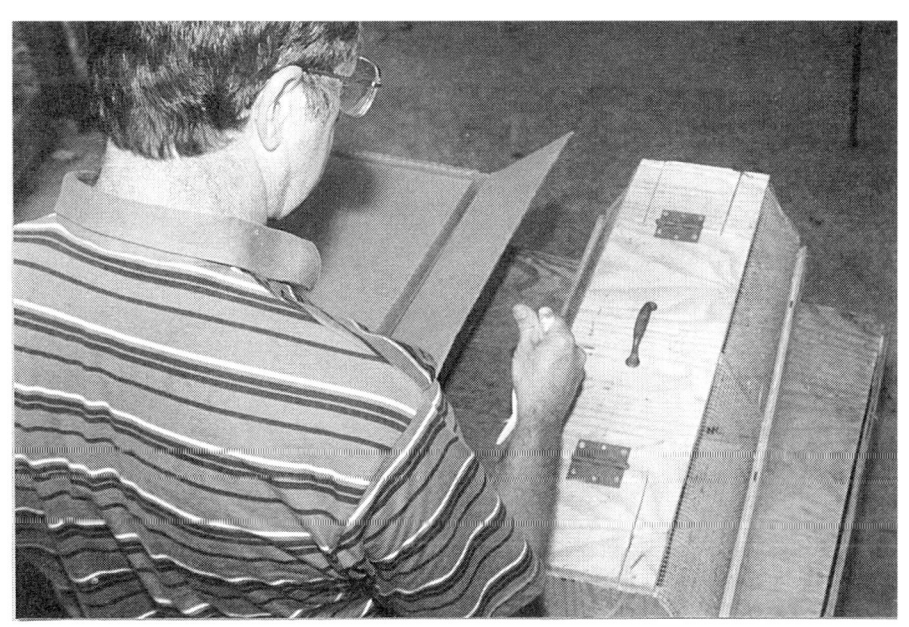

and immediately get a feel for the overall condition of the bird.

The greatest backyard business ever!

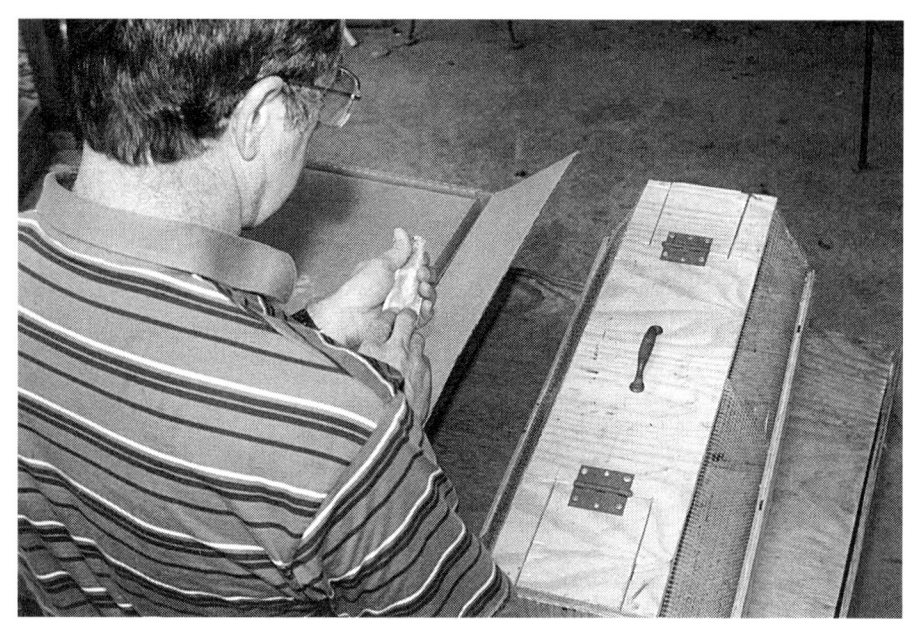

Transferring the bird to the left hand,

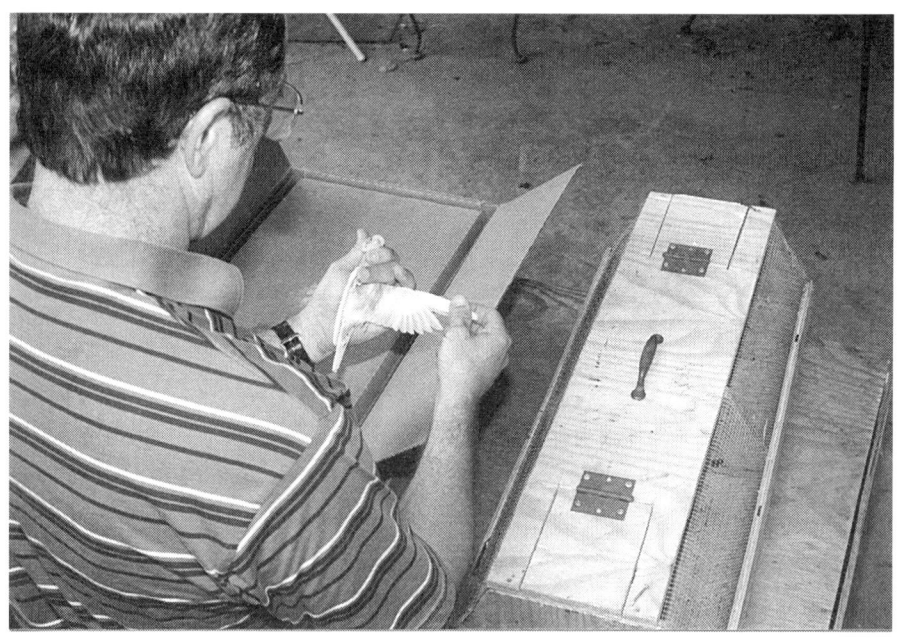

while quickly checking for multiple defects.

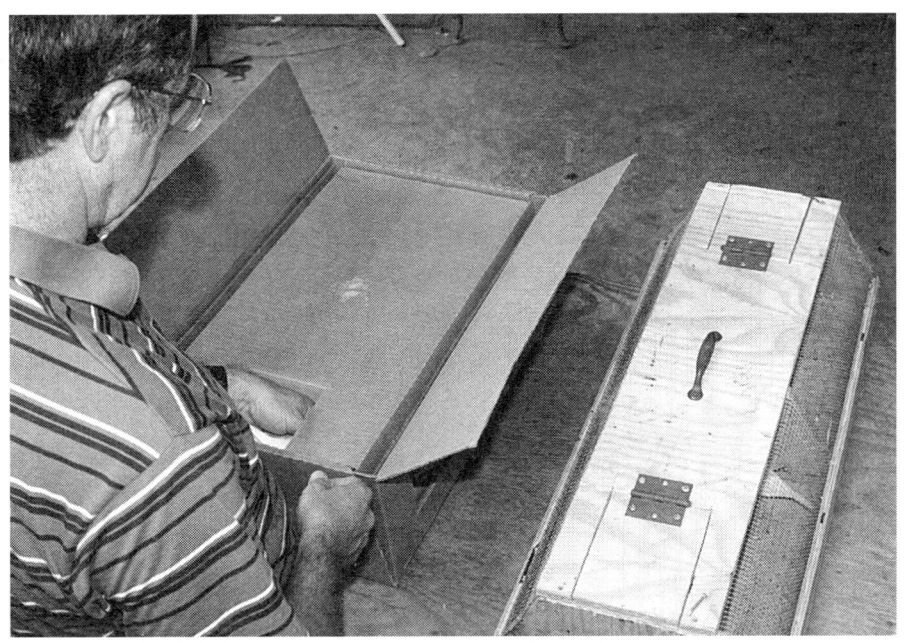

If the bird makes the grade, it goes into the shipping crate.

In this position you can check the:
- *Beak for deformities*
- *Feet for missing toes*
- *Eyes*
- *Nostrils, for signs of nasal discharge*
- *Vent, for signs of diarrhea*
- *Feathers*

The greatest backyard business ever!

Actually, your breeders should not bring birds that they know you will not buy, so 95% of the birds you receive should be buyable. Some of our better breeders would hardly ever bring a bird in that we would have to turn back. If they brought in 300 birds, we usually bought 300, unless they had accidentally let one slip by. On the other hand, there would be some who would always be bringing in their culls mixed in with the good ones, always trying to slip something past you. I guess that's just the nature of some people. You should grade those people's birds twice as hard. You just don't need birds or people like that. Educate your breeders so they will know what to bring; it will make your job much easier.

There sometimes is a market for B-grade birds, which are just birds with mild defects such as missing toes or a few feathers, but there is NO market for sickly birds. Some shops will run a special where they will give a bird away with the purchase of a cage, often times using B-grade birds for that.

As you will learn, birds will bite. Although parakeets can bite pretty hard, lovebirds, and especially cockatiels can take a chunk out of your hand. Therefore you must learn how to handle them properly, which just takes time. Rarely have I seen people use gloves with parakeets, but I have not infrequently seen people use gloves with lovebirds and cockatiels. When I see someone using gloves with any bird from the size of a cockatiel on down, I can't help but to think that they don't know much about birds. I don't know much about snakes, but if I saw a snake handler using gloves to handle snakes, I would just have to figure that he was an amateur and didn't know very much about handling snakes. I feel the same way when I see people handling birds with gloves. I just don't believe they know much about how to handle them. When you use gloves to handle small birds with, you simply cannot get a good feel for the bird and the possibility of injuring the bird is increased.

Shipping Your Birds

As a breeder, it will depend on how you market your birds as to whether or not you will be directly involved with shipping. But if you plan to become a wholesale distributor who markets birds on a national level, you will be heavily involved with the shipping process and it will pay you to learn it well. Your success will depend on it. Although it is by no means a complicated process, there are some definite rules that you will need to learn and abide by. You will learn that as a shipper of livestock, you are totally dependent on the airline industry. The different carriers have different rules and requirements for shipping different types of livestock, and the employees who work the counters where you will drop your birds off at will have a tendency to interpret the rules somewhat differently. In other words, a lot of them don't know how to interpret their own company policy. That's a fact. At the airport from which you ship, it will be to your advantage to establish a strong rapport with the counter employees at the freight terminals of the different airlines, as they will sometimes bend the rules a little to accommodate you if you are of the friendly sort.

I cannot over state the importance of shipping only healthy birds. It is almost impossible to ship a large shipment of birds, say 500 to 1000 birds, without having a few losses, but as a shipper we never incurred any heavy losses during our years in the business, and we shipped somewhere around a million birds, maybe more. By knowing how to ship and shipping only the healthiest of birds, your losses will be held at a minimum. In our many years of shipping, we never filed a claim with any airline.

Some shippers have a reputation of filing claims with the airlines for birds that arrive dead. I have known some unethical people to ship birds that were on the brink of death, and of course, those birds would not hold up to the stress of shipping and would arrive at their destination dead. Naturally, they would have declared a very high value on the birds at the time of shipment in order to collect from the airline. I knew of one airline that finally refused to accept birds from one particular shipper because of the amount of claims the shipper had filed with them over the course of time. Shippers like that are bad for the industry and everyone else is penalized for their actions, by increased freight rates and over zealous regulations. Again, ship only healthy birds.

Shipping Crates

Most shipping crates for small birds are made of cardboard and are of a throw away design. Bird shipping crates are not a common item, so you may have to get a corrugated box company to design and manufacture them for you. Fortunately, there are some companies that specialize in small orders of 500 boxes or so. The company that designed and manufactured our boxes was Specialty Container Corporation, 1608 Plantation Road, Dallas, Texas 75235. Our boxes measured 23" long, 15" wide and 7" tall and had screen wire covered window openings along both sides. Cockatiels and lovebirds like to chew, so in addition to the screen wire we would cover the window openings with hardwire cloth if we were shipping those type birds, since they could chew through the screen wire.

The 15" wide dimension was at the bottom of the box and it tapered to 13" at the top, making the top of the box 2" narrower than the bottom. That meant that if the boxes were stacked close together, since they had slopping sides, there was always a crack between them so as to allow airflow for ventilation. I have seen other bird shipping boxes that had straight sides on them in which 1 inch spacer blocks were glued to the sides of the box to make sure that the boxes couldn't be stacked so closely together that the ventilation was cut off. Whatever your design, make sure that the boxes will have adequate ventilation if stacked closely together. Boxes packed full of birds put off a lot of heat, and adequate ventilation is a must. I cannot over stress that point.

As a shipper, when you drop your birds off at the airport they are out of your control. When they are loaded in the belly of an aircraft, they are sometimes stacked as close together as they can get them, and if the box is not designed properly, the birds will suffocate.

You must also use common sense when packing your birds for shipment. Too many birds in a box will create problems and too few birds will cost your customer more in freight. Freight cost are usually paid by the receiver and not the shipper, but if you are to build a long term relationship with your customer, you will need to save them all the money that you can. Airlines will charge which ever figures the heaviest, the actual weight or the dimensional weight of the box. To figure dimensional weight, multiply the inches of the 3 dimensions. Our boxes measured 23"x15"x7"=2415 cubic inches. Different airlines use different figures to calculate how many cubic inches are in a pound. They will range anywhere from 192 cubic inches to 160 cubic inches per pound. The carrier that we used the most often figured it at 192 cubic inches per pound. Since our shipping boxes contained 2415 cubic inches, they were calculated as follows. 2415 divided by 192, therefore, they dimmed out at 12.5 lbs. per box. That meant that my customer was going to be charged for at least 12 ½ pounds per box, regardless of how much it weighed, even if it was an empty box.

We would use a 1 pound coffee can as a scoop, and usually put 1 ½ cans of feed per box. The shipping box, with feed included and 50 parakeets would weigh approximately 8 pounds. So you can see that our customer was always charged by the dimensional weight rather than the actual weight. It made no difference if there were 50 parakeets in the box or 5, the freight was going to be based on the rate of 12 ½ pounds per box, therefore, knowing how to pack your birds is of utmost importance in order to save your customer money.

When packing the birds for shipment, always try to fill the boxes to capacity to keep your customer from excessive freight charges. It is best to not mix the different types of birds in a box without a partition to divide them. For instance, if a customer only orders 6 cockatiels, don't put them in a box by themselves unless it

The greatest backyard business ever!

is a smaller box. Instead, you can partition off a section of the box and include them in the same box with other birds.

Birds ship much better in cool weather than hot weather, since they themselves put off a lot of heat in the shipping crates. Taking that into consideration, birds can be packed heavier in cooler weather than in hot weather. You must take into consideration the temperature at both the shipping and receiving end. For instance, when I was shipping birds from Dallas to Detroit, the Dallas temperature might be 80 degrees and the Detroit temperature 40 degrees. Therefore, we had to pack the birds for the warmer temperature. The following is based on the size of the shipping boxes we used and should be only used as a guideline.

Number of birds per crate in warm weather with box measuring 23"x15"x7".

Parakeets...40
Finches...60 to 70
Lovebirds...30
Cockatiels...15

Number of birds per crate in cool weather with box measuring 23"x15"x7".

Parakeets...40-60
Finches..... 60-80
Lovebirds... 30-40
Cockatiels....15-20

All things must be taken into consideration. How long the flight, whether or not it is a non-stop flight, temperature at both ends, etc. You will learn to adjust your shipping times to accommodate the temperature, when necessary. For instance, it is often necessary to ship during the middle of the night or very early mornings during the summer months when temperatures are extremely hot. Winter months often call for shipping in the heat of the day.

Your shipping crate must be labeled "Live Birds-Rush" along with "Allow For Ventilation" printed in bold letters down both sides of the box. Each box should be printed with your return address and phone number on it. Often times, when picking up other birds or animals at an airport, someone from another pet store other than the one you are shipping to will write that information down for future use. A number of times through the years I have had people call up and say that they had got my number off of our shipping crates at the airport and they were looking for a steady source of birds. A good looking, well designed shipping crate can be beneficial in developing future business.

We rarely ever shipped birds with water included in the crate. Instead, in each box we would normally include a sliced up orange, apple, or several stalks of celery, depending on which was the least expensive. If the birds were to be left in the crate for any extended period of time, I would sometimes put a small covered deli container, such as what ice cream or the like would come in, with a hole cut in the top of the cover where the birds could drink. Its important that you use a dish that has a cover with a hole cut in it, as the opening in the top of the dish does not need to be as large as the dish itself, or the birds will splash all the water out and ruin the cardboard shipping crate. A sponge or piece of foam rubber placed in the water will help keep it from sloshing out. Prior to shipping, remove the container and replace it with fruit or vegetables. During shipment, the fruit or vegetables seemed to work better than water and allowed the birds to get the moisture they needed without soaking the cardboard shipping box. Finches in particular need lots of fluids, and much more so in hot weather, so be sure to include an ample supply when shipping them.

The greatest backyard business ever!

*Note the tapered design of the box. Birds put off a lot of heat, so it is very important that shipping crates be well ventilated.
Boxes should be well labeled.*

Although these four boxes only weigh 32 pounds, the dimensional weight would figure to be 50 pounds and that is what the airline would charge for.

Shipping Requirements

In most instances, you will need to make reservations for your birds on a particular flight. It's just a simple matter of calling the freight department of the airline you are going to use. As you build your customer base, you will in most probability ship to the same customers over and over and will soon learn what flights work best. Always try to use non-stop flights whenever possible. You will also learn that in most cases, it is difficult or impossible to book animal shipments around the major holidays. That is because of the increase in passenger loads as well as the increase in the amount of mail the airlines are carrying. Normally, from about 10 days before Christmas till after the first of the year it is next to impossible to ship birds. If at all possible, ship early in the day and early in the week.

Airlines as well as the USDA impose temperature requirements in shipping livestock. USDA requirements are that the temperature on both ends of the shipment range somewhere between 45 and 85 degrees. Most airline requirements are the same. Many airlines will accept birds that are outside of those ranges if you provide them with a letter of acclimation, stating that the birds can handle higher or lower temperatures. Some airlines also have a higher priority service, such as counter-to-counter service that will accept livestock during extreme weather, provided they meet certain requirements. These are airline specific requirements and you would be better informed to check with whatever airline you are planning on using to get the latest requirements.

Some requirements originate from state regulations and some are requirements that the airlines themselves impose. Some states require health certificates and some don't. A few airlines will require a health certificate for all shipments, regardless of the state requirement. I think this is done out of ignorance, as the airline employees cannot interpret the various laws, and most health certificates are somewhat of a joke anyway. A health certificate can

The greatest backyard business ever!

be issued for a shipment of thousands of birds. How can a veterinarian tell which birds are healthy and which are not, unless they inspect each bird, which is next to impossible. And of course, health certificates can be duplicated or falsified in any number of ways. I want to again repeat, as a shipper you should be able to recognize a sickly bird much easier and quicker than a veterinary issuing a health certificate, since you are the one who packed them, and never, under any circumstances, should you ship one. Your requirements, standards and ethics should be as high or higher than what's required by some health certificate.

The various state requirements are far too many to list. USDA maintains a website, www.aphis.usda.gov./vs/sregs where you can find the different state requirements with the click of a mouse. They also have a toll free number, 1-800-545-8732 where you can use a voice response system to get the requirements of each individual state. Many states don't require anything at all, while some require state permits or health certificates.

Shipping C.O.D vs. Open Account

Most of our established customers were on an open account basis with us. Just as any other business would require, before you ship to a new customer on open account, you will want a list of several credit references to check out. Shipping C.O.D. is costly to your customer, as well as a lot of trouble. However, if he doesn't pay, it is costly to you. Therefore, check them out thoroughly before shipping very large orders open account. If they are a worthy customer and you are unwilling to ship open account orders, it will be hard to retain them for long. Just be sure to have an understanding with them that you need your money sent to you within what ever time frame you are willing to allow. Most of our customers ordered on a weekly or bi-weekly basis and I required them to only have one invoice out at a time, although it was not uncommon to have to call them to remind them to put the check in the mail. Your goal is to build a customer base of quality customers who will order from you on a regular basis. You will soon learn who is good pay, who is slow pay, etc. and what to expect.

The Delivery Van or Truck

As a wholesale distributor or breeder, if you deliver a volume of birds to either the airport or any other location, you will need a means of transportation that will offer an acceptable level of comfort to your birds, as well as yourself. It would not be uncommon for us to carry from 1000 to 3000 birds to the airport on our shipping days. That many birds confined in a small place can create a lot of heat, as well as a lot of dust. Most dealers I knew who were volume shippers used a van with a rear air conditioner as their delivery vehicle. The van worked well for the birds, but I found the comfort level for the driver to be unacceptable because of the extreme amount of dust in the air. Our delivery vehicle consisted of a long wheel base pickup truck with an aluminum camper shell on it. A one inch thick piece of styrofoam insulation was laid flat in the bed of the pickup, then a sheet of plywood was laid on top of that. This insulated the bottom of the bed from the extreme road heat that Texas summers produced. Another sheet of styrofoam insulation covered by a sheet of paneling was screwed to the top of the camper shell to insulate the top. An air conditioning shop installed a rear air conditioner in the back of the pickup truck. This allowed me to keep the back of the pickup at whatever temperature I wanted it at and I could stay comfortable in the front of the cab without the dust or noise associated with the large volume of birds in the back. It worked great.

The greatest backyard business ever!

Part III

Chapter 8
Breeding Birds
Colony Breeding vs. Cage Breeding

Colony breeding is normally defined as having a group or "colony" of birds in a large cage or flight pen, whereby cage breeding normally consists of having one pair of birds per cage. Both colony and cage breeding have their own distinct advantages and disadvantages, of which I will list a few. After you decide on which species of bird you would like to begin with, your next decision must be whether or not to cage or colony breed, as your building requirements will depend on which method you choose. The hookbill birds such as parakeets, cockatiels and lovebirds will gnaw or chew through the interior walls of your building unless they are covered with plywood that is at least 3/8 of an inch thick, whereas with cage breeding the interior wall construction is not as important, although plywood is my overall choice of wall covering. The amount of income you wish to derive from the breeding of birds, the amount of time you can devote to your breeding operation, as well as the size of your building or space in which you can construct a building are all factors that you will need to consider before making your decision as to whether to use cages or colonies with your breeding operation.

With cage breeding, you can put more birds in a given area than you can with colony breeding. Using parakeets as an example, in colony breeding a good rule of thumb is to allow 1 square foot of floor space per bird. For instance, a building that has 1000 square feet of floor space divided into breeding pens would allow enough space for 500 pair of birds. That same building would accommodate from 800 to 1000 pair of birds in breeding cages, depending on how the cages were arranged.

The greatest backyard business ever!

Many birds are territorial and will fight quite a bit if they are overcrowded in a flight. Parakeets are particularly bad about fighting if overcrowded and not only will they fight, but they will often go into another nest box and kill the other birds nestlings if crowded too much. Provided you have a bonded pair, the fighting problem is eliminated with cage breeding. Because there is less fighting, the production level of cage breeding is usually higher than colony breeding. Another factor worth noting is that with colony breeding, if you have 40 pair of parakeets in a colony, as a general rule there will usually only be around 75% of the birds that will actually be breeding and raising babies, as the other birds will simply not find a mate that they will bond with. With a colony, it is difficult to determine which birds are breeding and which ones are not, therefore you will always have a percentage of birds that are not breeding and you simply can't tell which ones they are. With cage breeding, if the birds you have paired up are not breeding, you will know it and you can re-mate them with other birds in an effort to get 100% of the birds working.

Advantages of cage breeding.

- Less fighting
- More birds per building
- Higher percentage of birds working
- More production per pair
- More income per building
- Better control of genetics and colors produced
- You can tell what birds are not breeding
- Easier to control disease
- Birds will normally go to breeding at an earlier age in cages

Disadvantages of cage breeding

- More labor intensive
- Initial setup cost can be a little higher

Advantages of colony breeding
- Less labor intensive
- Initial cost is slightly lower

Disadvantages of colony breeding
- More fighting between breeding birds
- Higher percentage of non-breeding birds
- Difficult to control genetics and colors produced
- Less production per pair
- Less production per building
- Less profit per building
- Harder to control disease

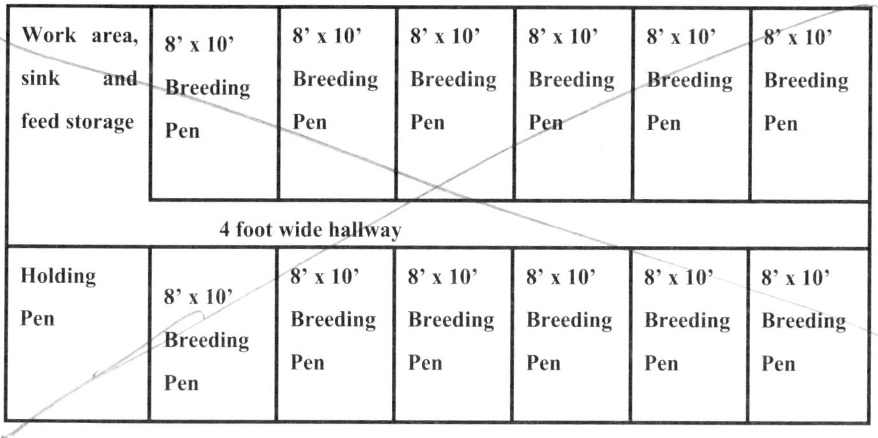

Work area, sink and feed storage	8' x 10' Breeding Pen	8' x 10' Breeding Pen	8' x 10' Breeding Pen	8' x 10' Breeding Pen	8' x 10' Breeding Pen	8' x 10' Breeding Pen
4 foot wide hallway							
Holding Pen	8' x 10' Breeding Pen	8' x 10' Breeding Pen	8' x 10' Breeding Pen	8' x 10' Breeding Pen	8' x 10' Breeding Pen	8' x 10' Breeding Pen

The above diagram is of one of our parakeet colony breeding buildings that was later converted to cage breeding. This building has 12 flight pens for breeding that each contain 80 square feet of floor space, enough space for 40 pair of parakeets in each pen. The building would house approximately 480 to 500 pair of parakeets. The same building, as you can see in the drawing below, will easily handle approximately 1000 to 1100 pair of parakeets in breeding cages if they are arranged properly.

The greatest backyard business ever!

Handwritten annotations around diagram:

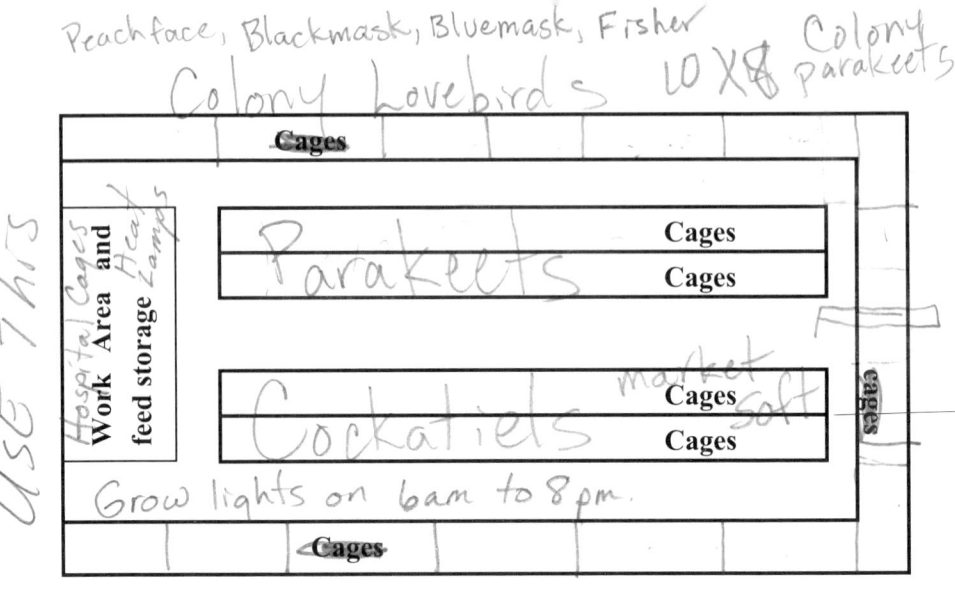

Top: Peachface, Blackmask, Bluemask, Fisher — Colony Lovebirds 10 X 8 — Colony parakeets

Left side: USE THIS

Inside diagram (left box): Hospital Cages, Work Area and feed storage, Heat Lamps

Inside diagram: Parakeets — Cockatiels — market soft

Below diagram: Grow lights on 6am to 8pm.

Bottom: Colony Finches from PuertoRico 10 X 8 Colony

Diagram labels: Cages (top, sides, bottom)

24' x 56' building used for cage breeding of parakeets

For colony breeding, we used the following square footage of floor space per bird as a guideline.

- Parakeets 1 square foot of floor space per bird
- Cockatiels 5 square foot of floor space per bird
- Lovebirds 1 1/2 square foot of floor space per bird
- Zebra finches .6 (6/10) square foot of floor space per bird

We have found an 8' x 10' pen to be the ideal size for colony breeding, regardless of the type of bird. Using the above figures, we would put 40 pair of parakeets, 8 pair of cockatiels, 25 pair of lovebirds, or 65 pair of zebra finches in an 8' x 10' breeding pen. You can deviate from these figures a little, but it has been our experience that by putting more birds in a pen, it will create a more stressful environment, with the net result being less offspring per pen instead of more.

Many of the larger commercial parakeet breeders use the cage breeding system. Cockatiel and lovebird breeders seem to be split as to what works best, cages or colonies. Zebra finches seem to do much better in colonies than in cages. My own personal experience is that

I like cage breeding for parakeets and cockatiels, and colony breeding for lovebirds and zebra finches.

Two exceptionally nice cage breeding operations.

Cockatiels being raised in a colony.

A nice colony of parakeets.

Housing Requirements

Whether you decide to raise parakeets, cockatiels, lovebirds or finches, the housing requirements will be about the same. The exception to that rule would be if you were only going to raise finches. Parakeets, cockatiels and lovebirds bred in colonies will gnaw or chew through the interior walls of your building if they are covered with anything less than 3/8 inch thick plywood, whereas finches will not. If you are building a new building, regardless of what you plan to raise, I would suggest you cover the interior walls with plywood that is at least 3/8 inch thick.

Your geographical location will also play a roll in what type of building you will need. Common sense will tell you that someone living in southern Florida will obviously require a different type of building than someone living in Green Bay, Wisconsin, or Minot, North Dakota.

By no means is it necessary to construct a new building. I have known people to successfully raise birds in practically any type of building, provided it meets certain criteria. Mobile homes, portable storage buildings, enclosed garages, and basements have all been successfully used in breeding exotic birds. Normally, an existing building can be remodeled and adapted to the raising of birds quite easily.

If you plan to breed your birds in colonies, the partitions in your pens should be made of ½" x 1" welded wire or ½"x ½" hardware cloth. Personally, I like the welded wire the best, although it is a little more expensive than the hardware cloth. If the building has windows in it, they should be covered with ¼ inch hardware cloth to keep mice out. As hard as it sounds, mice can actually get through the ½" x 1" welded wire or ½"x ½" hardware cloth if it is used to cover windows.

Of course, concrete floors are best, but buildings with wood floors will work fine. Just don't try to use a building with a dirt floor. It won't work, as rodents will tunnel under the walls and into the building. Dirt also creates an ideal environment for parasites.

Be sure that the walls and ceilings of the building are well insulated, because insulation is far cheaper in the long run than heating and cooling bills.

The greatest backyard business ever!

Climate Control and Ventilation

Although most birds can take a very wide range of temperatures, they will do best between about 65 and 85 degrees. However, the best rule of thumb is that it should be comfortable for you. If you are comfortable, then the birds will be comfortable also. Your means of heating and cooling will probably be determined by your geographical location as well as the design of the building you are using. Our buildings were heated with propane heaters in the winter and cooled with water fans in the summer. If outside temperature permitted, the windows would be opened to allow fresh air and ventilation.

Central heat and air is probably the best if you have a large building. If you use central heat and air, you will need to change your filter often, depending on the amount of birds in the building. A building packed to capacity with birds will put off quite a bit of dust, and the central heat and air unit will help keep the dust to a minimum, provided that you change the filter often. Washable filters are available and can be re-used over and over. An exhaust fan or two in one end of the building will also cut down on the amount of dust in a building, which is important for both the birds as well as yourself.

Some parts of the country have such a mild climate that no heating or cooling at all is required, although most locations will require at least some of one or the other.

A nice building used for colony breeding parakeets. It is designed to allow the birds to go outside when the weather permits.

Buildings designed to breed birds in do not have to be fancy, just efficient. The above setup is used to breed cockatiels, finches and parakeets in colonies. You can tell that it has been added on to several times, indicating a profitable business.

A small setup designed for cage breeding.

The greatest backyard business ever!

This building is used for cage breeding parakeets. It is well insulated and requires practically no heating or cooling, even though it is located in north Texas.

These 3 brick bird buildings were built to match the owner's house. They are used to colony breed lovebirds.

These are great little buildings to use when first starting

Lighting Requirements

Some years back I was told by Dr. Fred Thornberry, a professor at the poultry science department at Texas A & M University, that there was more known about a chicken than any other living creature on the face of the earth. He said that the chicken was the most thoroughly researched animal in existence and that there simply wasn't anything more to learn about a chicken. With that, one can safely conclude that the lighting requirements of poultry have been extensively studied and are well known, and poultry raisers have used that knowledge to their benefit to dramatically increase production levels. Although the pet birds we are raising today are not the same as poultry, some of the same principals that apply to poultry can apply to the raising of these birds, and lighting is definitely one of them.

The reproductive activity of all domestic birds and many wild ones is influenced by light. Until late in the 19th century, people generally thought egg production was seasonal, although for hundreds of years the Japanese had used candles to influence caged songbirds. With natural lighting, birds build nests and lay eggs in the spring, stop nesting and go into a molt in the fall. When man learned that the proper use of light could make the hen react as if it was springtime all year, fresh eggs soon became available year-round.

While hatching in the spring and early summer, growing in late summer and early fall, resting during the winter and coming into production in the early spring works well for the light-influenced wild birds, this natural system doesn't satisfy the commercial poultry producers, nor should it satisfy the commercial pet bird producer. The natural light schedules also slow the development of birds that will be used for future breeding purposes, therefore, artificial light should be used by the commercial producer of pet birds who wants to achieve maximum results.

Scientist do not completely understand the mechanisms by which birds respond to light. However, we do know that light generally causes the bird to become active, to eat, and to drink. It

The greatest backyard business ever!

also stimulates the bird's endocrine system. Light stimulates a series of events directly connected with the rate of sexual maturity or activity. Light affects the development of the growing birds in a positive manner, thus allowing them to mature considerably earlier than they would under normal seasonal conditions, and stimulates the reproductive systems of both the male and female birds.

Generally, birds do not need extremely bright lights as they see better in dim light than people do. If the lights are too bright, birds can become nervous and your results will not be as good as with a lower level of light. Normal household lighting is best. If you can read a newspaper well, that is about the right amount of light in the building.

Although ordinary incandescent light bulbs are the cheapest, they have a relatively short life and do not use electricity very efficiently. Florescent lights are more costly than incandescent lights, but use less electricity and last much longer than incandescent bulbs. The best results can be achieved with the type of fluorescent light bulbs that are nearest to sunlight spectrum, such as those used in greenhouses. All lighting systems should operate on an automatic timer for your convenience.

For maximum production from your birds, give them about 14 hours of light per day. If your birds are housed in buildings with windows, you will need to check the seasonal day length and adjust the amount of supplemental light provided. In buildings with windows, supplemental light should be added in the morning hours with the lighting then turned off later in the day, allowing the birds to go to roost when the natural light dims at dusk.

Bird producers with birds in windowless houses can plan any lighting schedule while those using houses with windows must plan lighting schedules around the days length. If you have a windowless house, you will need to have your lights set up on two different circuits, with a timer on each circuit. This will allow you to set the timers so that part of the lights turn off about 30 minutes before the rest of the lights go off, so as to simulate a sunset by gradually darkening the building. That is very important, because the birds need to feed their babies as well as themselves before going to roost. In buildings with no windows, a dim night-light needs to be provided.

Lighting is but one of the ways that you can really increase your production. Just remember, the laying hen needs to be thought of as a very finely tuned machine and she should not be subjected to day-to-day variations in the lighting schedule. Take the subject of lighting seriously and make any changes gradually, instead of sudden.

Rodents

One of the most important of all things to consider is that your building must be as rat and mouse proof as possible. If you are wanting this to become a profitable venture, as I am sure you are, you will need to remember that you just simply cannot raise birds and mice in the same building.

Because the birds are grain eaters, mice will be attracted to the building because of the grain inside. By keeping the area outside of the building clean and junk free, mice and rats will not have a hiding place and the likely- hood of a big infestation is decreased. All cracks or holes in the exterior walls must be sealed, or mice as well as rats and snakes can enter the walls of the building. Mice and rats will then cut through the interior walls and get into the building itself. Mice become active at night, and will create havoc with your birds, often causing the adult birds to abandon their nest boxes which may be full of babies or eggs. Keeping the inside of the building tidy and clutter free is also very important, as it will decrease the places for mice to hide.

We always kept several catch alive mouse traps set in each building to alert us if we were having a mouse problem. Our buildings were as mouse proof as one can make a building, but once in a while a mouse would still show up inside the building, possibly coming in with a load of feed. But the catch alive traps would let us know if we were having a mouse problem. Since mice are usually only active at dark, it is not uncommon for a breeder to have a mouse problem and

The greatest backyard business ever!

not know it, other than the fact that his or her production is down. I just cannot over emphasize this point-you cannot successfully raise birds and mice in the same building. Make your building as mouse proof as possible.

Nutrition

Exotic birds are not recognized as having the same economic value as do chickens, turkeys, and some species of gamebirds, and until recently, there has been very little scientific research done on the nutritional requirements of these birds in comparison to other types of fowl. The poultry industry is a well organized multi-billion dollar industry that has funded major studies at the poultry science departments of the leading universities and research centers in the nation. In addition, many of the leading feed companies themselves have spent huge sums of money studying the feeding requirements of poultry, as the poultry feed business itself is also a multi-billion dollar industry, whereas the exotic bird feed business is a much smaller segment of their overall business.

The exotic bird industry itself is highly fragmented, mostly unorganized and under funded, with the net result being that very little scientific knowledge is known about the actual nutritional requirements of the various individual species. The past few years has, however, seen an increasing amount of research conducted in the area of avian nutrition, with the formulation of several pelleted feeds that are now on the market. Some of these are simply based on the known nutritional requirements of poultry and gamebirds, while others are in fact, based on actual research conducted with exotic birds. It would be great if there was a commercial feed available on the market today that was in a pelleted form, that was completely balanced and contained all the essential elements necessary for optimal growth, maintenance, and breeding of exotic birds, that was affordable, that the birds would readily accept, and that you could see positive results in the form of increased production of healthy offspring. While we are now learning more about the nutritional requirements of exotic birds, there still are a number of hurdles to clear before the commercial raiser converts from their known, proven feeding programs to the pelleted diets that the poultry industry enjoys.

Parakeets, cockatiels, lovebirds and zebra finches are all considered to be finicky or picky eaters. In other words, they are not quick to change their eating habits. This is especially true with the older birds. In fact, some birds will literally starve to death before they will accept something new, such as a pelleted feed. Therefore, it makes no difference how good the feed is, if the bird won't eat it, it is of no value. Another factor that is not in favor of the pelleted feeds on the market today is the cost factor. For a commercial breeder who has hundreds or perhaps thousands of pairs of small birds, it is cost prohibitive to feed the pelleted feeds that are currently available today. I do not know if it is price gouging or what, but pelleted feeds manufactured for exotic birds range from two to three dollars a pound, whereas poultry feed, which is very similar in content, can be purchased for less than fifteen cents per pound. I cannot help but to believe that since a chicken sells for a couple of dollars and a parrot sells for a couple of hundred dollars, that the companies manufacturing, promoting and selling the pelleted feeds for exotic birds have used this price difference to their advantage when setting the price of their exotic bird pelleted feed.

Another negative of the pelleted feeds is that they most often create large amounts of wet stools in the young nestlings, which in turn makes for a wet, fouled nest box, often resulting in droppings that stick to and deform the feet of the nestlings. Although the pelleted feeds available today for exotic birds may, no doubt, be suited for the larger birds such as parrots and macaws, where the breeder doesn't house hundreds of pairs, and where the breeder removes the babies from the nestbox and handraises them, they are not widely used by commercial breeders of parakeets, cockatiels, lovebirds and zebra finches because of the above mentioned reasons.

Since we don't know the exact nutritional requirements of parakeets, cockatiels, lovebirds and zebra finches, and since these birds are essentially seedeaters, we must therefore feed a variety of seeds and supplemental feeds in order to attempt to meet their essential nutritional needs.

The following is the average nutritional analysis of the various seeds and grains most often found in bird feed mixes or supplements. These averages can vary considerably, based on the season in which the crops were harvested, the age and stage the crop was in when harvested, time since crop was harvested as well as the storage conditions, type of soil the crop was grown in, whether or not it was fertilized, the amount of rainfall, etc.

Average Nutritional Analysis

Seed	% Protein	% Fat	% Fiber
Millet, white	11.6	3.5	6.5
Millet, red	11.6	3.5	6.5
Millet, yellow	11.7	3.3	8.0
Canary seed	16.6	5.9	6.0
Oat groats	12.3	7.0	2.0
Sunflower	16.0	25.6	28.0
Safflower	15.6	31.6	25.7
Rape seed	22.9	38.4	6.0
Flax	23.0	34.5	6.0
Niger	19.0	41.5	9.0
Sesame	21.1	42.0	5.0
Corn	8.5	3.0	3.0
Wheat	10.5	1.5	4.0

Exotic birds need to be fed a blend of various seeds in order to provide a wider a range of nutrients. The following table lists protein, fat and fiber percentages of seed blends that are commercially available and have been used successfully to raise millions of parakeets, cockatiels, lovebirds and zebra finches. Make sure that the seed blends that you use falls within these ranges.

Species	% Protein in most seed blends	% Fat	% Fiber
Parakeets	13-16	5-6	5-7
Cockatiels	12-14	9-11	9-12
Lovebirds	12-14	9-11	9-12
Zebra finches	13-16	4-7	5-7

When grain is harvested, it goes through a cleaning process that removes much of the dust and foreign material. It is important that exotic birds be fed as clean and dust free grain as you can get. The better quality grains are triple cleaned, and will have a shiny, glossy look to them.

Labels on Feed Mixes

There are both federal and state laws that regulate the feed industry. The law requires that when feed is composed of more than one item, such as a blend of seeds that make up a parakeet mix, that the bag be labeled. In addition to federal requirements, most states will require a guaranteed analysis as well as a list of the ingredients to be printed on each bag of feed that is sold. Although the ingredients must be listed, the actual amounts of the various ingredients are not required to be listed, and rightfully so, since that would allow feed companies to copy each others formulas. However, the ingredients are required to be listed in descending order of predominance, according to the actual weight of each ingredient. Feed labels can be a little tricky and deceiving as the following story will show.

The greatest backyard business ever!

As a wholesale distributor of birds, we carried a full line of feed and supplies for the bird breeders in our area. We had two blends of parakeet mix that we carried, our McDonald's Standard Parakeet mix and McDonald's Deluxe parakeet mix.

McDonald's Standard Parakeet Mix consisted of:
65% white proso millet
25% canary seed
10% oat groats

Feed label read as follows:
Crude protein, Minimum 13%
Crude fat, Minimum 4%
Crude fiber, Minimum 6%
Moisture, Maximum 12%
Ingredients: White proso millet, canary seed, oat groats

Blend # 2
McDonald's Deluxe Parakeet Mix consisted of:
50% white proso millet
40% canary seed
10% oat groats

Feed label read as follows:
Crude protein, Minimum 14%
Crude fat, Minimum 5%
Crude fiber, Minimum 6%
Moisture, Maximum 12%
Ingredients: White proso millet, canary seed, oat groats.

As you can see, these two feeds appear very close on the label, although the Deluxe was a better quality feed. While the analysis of white proso millet and canary seed are very close, the canary seed is a much higher quality seed and apparently has a higher degree of digestible and usable proteins and other nutrients than does the white proso millet, since the birds will produce much better when fed mixes that contain higher percentages of canary seed. We have found, however, that mixes containing over 40% canary seed do not have any additional benefits.

A regional competitor in the feed business had a mix which they called "Protein Parakeet mix" and it consisted basically of the following.

Protein Parakeet mix consisted of:

80% white proso millet

10% canary seed

10% oat groats

This is a very low quality ration to feed to parakeets, since it consisted mostly of white proso millet. However, to each ton of this mix they added 50 pounds of chicken laying crumbles. Since chicken feed is less expensive than bird seed, this should have decreased the cost of the feed. But that wasn't the case. Bird producers who purchased this feed actually ended up paying higher prices for the chicken feed that was included in the mix than if they had purchased the chicken feed separately. Although chicken feed is balanced and contains all the nutrients that chickens need, parakeets will hardly touch it, and for the most part, it is a waste to include it in parakeet mix. But chicken feed does have a lot of ingredients in it that parakeet seed doesn't have, and adding it to a parakeet mix will certainly make a nice looking, impressive label as you can see by the following 53 items that the company could now legally list under the ingredients section of the feed label.

Feed Label read as follows:

Crude protein, Minimum 12%

Crude fat, Minimum 4%

Crude fiber, Minimum 6%

Moisture, Maximum 12%

The greatest backyard business ever!

Ingredients: White proso millet, canary seed, oat groats, corn meal, ground oats, corn chips, dehydrated alfalfa meal, wheat middlings, rice bran, plant protein products, dried whey, brewers dried yeast, yeast culture, roughage products, saccharomyces cervisiae yeast, dried lactobacillus acidophilus fermentation product, dried lactobacillus plantarum fermentation product, dried lactobacillus bulgaricus fermantation product, dried lactobacillus lactis fermentation product, dried enterococcus cremoris fermentation product, dried enterococcus diacetylactis fermentation product, dried bacillus subtillis fermentation product, dried aspergillus oryzae fermentation extract, dried aspergillus niger fermentation product, dried milk protein, dried colostrum milk product, lecithin, wheat germ oil, soybean oil, dl-methionine, l-lysine, vitamin a supplement(Stability Improved) Vitamin D3 supplement, vitamin e supplement, choline chloride, riboflavin supplement, niacin supplement, calcium pantothenate, Folic acid, Pyridoxide hydrochloride, vitamin b-12 supplement, Menadione Sodium Bisulfite complex(source of vitamin K activity), Monocalcium carbonate, calciym carbonate, potassium chloride, salt, magnesium oxide, ferrous sulfate, manganous oxide, copper sulfate, zinc sulfate, sodium selenite, and calcium iodate.

To the uninformed, this might appear to be a high quality parakeet ration, while in fact, it is a very poor quality mix. An 80/10/10 mix of millet, canary and oat groats is not at all a good balance of seed, and the addition of chicken feed doesn't help matters, especially since the birds don't eat the chicken feed. But the label sure looked impressive, and even the name "Protein Parakeet mix" sounds good. Bottom line, make sure you know what is in the feed you buy, that its good for your birds, and that they will eat it.

A cheap feed can often be the most expensive, in terms of lost production. Our main business was to breed, buy and sell birds, and our feed business was secondary to us, therefore, we refused to handle a cheap quality feed.

Supplements To The Diet

Total seed diets do not constitute a complete diet, regardless of the protein and fat content of the seed blend, as many seeds are deficient in essential nutrients. That being the case, in addition to the seed blend, a sound feeding program absolutely must include a supplemental feed mixture. There are a number of these high protein, vitamin-mineral supplements that are commercially available, such as Birds Choice, Petamine, Bird Booster, Nutricare, etc. Carrots and green leafy vegetables can also be fed in order to help supply essential vitamins and minerals.

The following tables list the major vitamins and minerals necessary for the generally accepted nutritional requirements in a birds diet, as well as the general biological functions and sources of food where the vitamins and minerals can be found.

Vitamin	Biological Functions	Sources
Vitamin A	Vitamin A is one of the most essential vitamins. Involved in carbohydrate, fat and protein metabolism, and general growth. Fertility, reproduction, and glandular functions.	Carrots, plant leaves and many dark green vegetables, eggs, alfalfa leaf meal.
Vitamin D the sunshine vitamin	Used in the regulation and utilization of calcium and phosphorus. It is important for skeletal bone growth, strength of bones, eggshell quality and prevention of certain diseases. Reproduction and viability of the young. Prevents rickets	Fish and beef livers, egg yolk, some animal fats.
Vitamin E	Muscle metabolism, fertility, growth, glandular health.	Wheat germ oil, seed germs, vegetable oils
Vitamin K	Blood clotting	Green leafy vegetables
Vitamin B complex	Promotes growth, appetite, blood and liver functions, fertility, and overall health of the heart and nerves.	Alfalfa leaf meal, various seeds and grains, liver, milk yeast, eggs

The greatest backyard business ever!

Mineral	Biological Functions	Sources
Vitamin C	Vitamin c is essential for production of the constituents of collagen, which is necessary for the growth of cartilage and bone.	Alfalfa leaf meal, vegetables, fruits
Vitamin F	Feather and skin health, blood clotting, overall health in young growing birds.	Oil seeds, wheat germ, alfalfa leaf meal
Calcium	Bone building, muscle, nerve and heart function. Production of eggshell. Blood component. Prevention of rickets. Reproduction	Milk, green ground bone meal, alfalfa leaf meal.
Phosphorus	Bone building, energy metabolism. Prevention of rickets. Reproduction.	Milk, Bone meal, meat and fish, cereals
Magnesium	Growth, reproduction, nerves and blood.	Dark green leafy vegetables, seeds, bone meal
Iron	Carrier of oxygen in the blood. Prevents anemia.	Eggs, dark green leafy vegetables, some grains and seeds, liver and heart.
Sodium and Potassium	Aids in normal growth and muscle function. Regulator of blood and body fluids.	Vegetables and table salt.
Chloride	Regulator of blood and body fluids.	Vegetables and table salt.
Sulfur	Growth, body regulation, feather production	Eggs and meat
Copper	Growth of red blood sells, bone formation, normal heart function and is essential in formation of hemoglobin synthesis and reproduction. Overall health.	Dark green leafy vegetables, yeast, some grains, organ meats.
Iodine	Thyroid health and normal growth.	Iodized salt, kelp, dairy products and

The principal use of food by birds, animals, and humans alike is as a source of energy, and the protein, fat, and carbohydrate content contained in the available food sources combine together to supply this energy. Entire books can be written on such complicated subjects as the twenty or so different amino acids that make up proteins, the different carbon sugars that are part of the structural makeup of carbohydrates, or the composition of the different fatty acids that make up fat in the diet.

Animal nutrition is a very complex science, and it is not the scope of this book to go into a detailed, in depth analysis of the subject. I have chosen, rather, to focus on successful feeding programs that have a proven record over time. I myself have used the feeding programs listed in this book to produce tens of thousands of birds, and having been a wholesale distributor of birds for many years, I have bought hundreds and hundreds of thousands of parakeets, cockatiels, lovebirds, and zebra finches from many individual raisers who used these same types of diets.

The importance of sound nutrition cannot be overemphasized. The poor results of an inadequate diet cannot be overcome by the best genetics in the world. An inadequate diet can lead to:

- Poor feathering
- Egg binding
- Smaller clutches of eggs
- Reduced hatchability
- Early chick mortality
- French molt
- Reproductive problems
- Rickets
- Fatty liver disease
- A shortened life span
- A weakened state that can lead to a whole host of diseases

Many birds or animals can be maintained on an inadequate diet for quite a long time, but to reproduce well, the lack of a sound diet spells disaster if you are in this business to make money.

Acquiring Your Breeding Stock

Your initial success or failure in the bird business can often be determined by the quality of birds that you start off with. Try to know some history about where your breed stock comes from and by all means, if at all possible go to see the breeding farm where they were produced.

If you do not plan to market your own birds and plan to sell to a bird buyer, if he is a reputable person, he should be able to get good quality birds for you. As a buyer, when we had people come to us who wanted to get into the business of raising birds, we would do everything possible to ensure their success, since our success as a wholesale distributor depended on their success in raising quality birds for us to sell. Because we bought their birds, we knew which breeders were raising the best quality birds and enjoying the best success rate. It was from those breeders that we would select the birds to sell to someone that was just starting out in the business. If one of our best breeders brought in, lets say, 600 birds a month, (the best birds don't necessarily come from the biggest raisers) and someone just starting out in the business wanted 100 pair of birds, it might take a couple of months to get the birds for them. Out of the 600 birds a month, you only select the cream of the crop for future breeding purposes, and in addition, you must try to select the colors that you know will sell the best in the future, plus, if at all possible, you try to select equal numbers of male and female birds. If you purchase your birds from an honest and reputable buyer, he or she should do everything possible to get you started off on the right tract with good quality birds.

Almost without exception, it is always best to start out with baby birds and let them grow to breeding age at your own facility. Many other animals can be moved from one environment to another

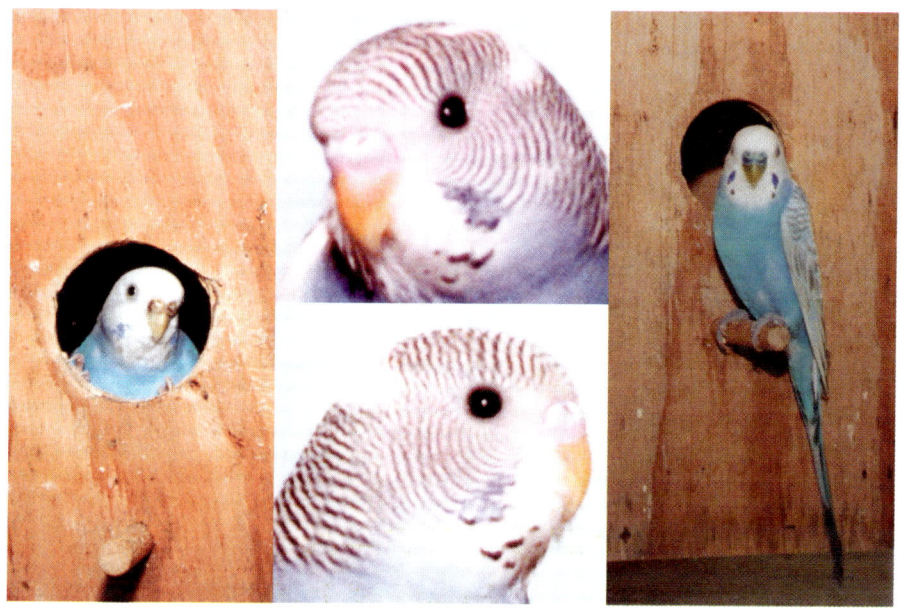

Color Plate #1. Sexing Parakeets. When the chicks hatch, the cere will be a pinkish or bluish color as in the middle pictures. As the bird matures, the cere of the female will turn a whitish, tanish or brown color as in the left photo. The cere of the male will usually turn blue or purple, although on the color mutations, it will sometimes remain pink.

Color Plate #2. Sexing cockatiels. Adult female cockatiels will have the bars on the underside of the wing. Males do not. Bars are harder to see on pieds, albinos, etc.

Normal cockatiel males have brightly colored heads.

Lengthening the amount of daylight hours by means of artificial lighting has long been used by the poultry industry to increase egg production. The same methods work well with exotic birds also. Florescent grow lights that are used in greenhouses produce a full spectrum of light that is almost equivalent to natural sunlight.

Although not an average size clutch, the above nest actually contained 11 baby chicks. When saving birds for replacement breeders, it is best to save chicks from your highest producers, since reproductive rates are an inheritable trait. The bottom nest only contained 3 chicks, with one egg that did not hatch.

Finches will nest in practically anything. The above photo is a 3' x 3' cage with several pairs of finches using wicker nest, while the bottom photo has homemade nestboxes.

Blackmask lovebirds   Bluemask lovebirds

Peachface lovebirds    Fisher lovebirds

Color Plate #3.... Most lovebirds are extremely difficult to visually distinguish between the sexes. Coloration alone is not a reliable factor, therefore a combination of characteristics must be used when sexing lovebirds.

Color plate#4. Sexing Zebra Finches. Color of beak indicates 2 males and 1 female in closest photo. Cheek patch and color of beak indicates 1 male and 1 female in photo on the far right.

A combination of beak coloration and other characteristics described on page 204 make sexing zebra finches almost 100% accurate. You should be able to easily distinguish males from females in the below photo. Note the black billed baby which is fresh out of the nestbox on the extreme right side of photo.

Most of the larger lovebird producers prefer to breed their birds in colonies.

James and Brenda McDonald with a shipment of birds. Birds can be shipped by airfreight to practically any major city. We usually shipped on a weekly basis, 50 weeks out of the year. The above shipment of birds will be in pet shops in New York within 12 hours after leaving our place in Texas.

Parakeets come in a rainbow of colors. Breeding for specific colors is an interesting and necessary part of a profitable bird business.

Cockatiels will breed well in cages or colonies. The above nestbox contains five eggs, which is about the average clutch size.

without any adverse effect on their breeding cycles. Not so with birds, as they are much more temperamental. It is not at all uncommon to move adult breeding age birds from one place to another and for them to never lay another egg. In addition, after a bird reaches adult status, it is difficult to tell the exact age of a bird. Many a newcomer to this business has been heart broken by buying adult birds and later finding out that they had bought somebody's wore out breeders. Don't run the risk, only start with baby birds.

All of the birds featured in this book come in a variety of colors. While some colors will usually bring more money than others, such as a pied or albino cockatiel vs. a normal gray cockatiel, I believe it is usually best to have an assortment of colors and not just the hottest selling color at the moment. By having an assortment, you will be assured of having at least some of the colors that are bringing the best prices at any given time.

If you purchase directly from a breeder, if at all possible, go and see their facility and try to determine the quality of birds they are producing. Only deal with someone who you feel you can believe and trust. That is especially true if you know very little about birds, which is the case with most people just getting in the business. Local feed stores that sell bird feed and supplies can sometimes help you to locate breeders in their area that you may be able to purchase breed stock from.

When breeding any type of bird or animal, the question of inbreeding invariably comes up. While I do not hold a degree in genetics, I have however, studied the subject somewhat extensively and successfully applied what I have learned to the breeding of numerous species of birds and animals. Inbreeding is merely a way of concentrating both the good qualities and/or the bad qualities that the subject already possesses. It is through inbreeding that man has been able to produce the fastest race horses, the cows who give the most milk, as well as the chickens that lay the most eggs. However, these achievements were not accomplished by starting with cull animals or birds. The animals with the best traits were selected and

The greatest backyard business ever!

the process started from there. It is for that reason that it is absolutely essential that you only start with the best birds from the best breeders in the business, if at all possible. And from there, you must always rigidly select and cull your offspring for future breeding purposes. Because of the possibility of bringing in a disease, it is usually best not to bring new birds into your flock once you are fully established. Therefore, when you need future breeders, "keep the best and sell the rest". Let that be your motto.

Chapter 9

Breeding Parakeets

Breeding Parakeets In Colonies

As discussed earlier in this book, I believe the best pen size for colony breeding any of the birds in this book is an 8' x 10' with an 8' ceiling. You can have as many pens in a building as your building size permits. The following diagrams are just included to give you an idea of a colony breeding layout. You can adapt your building to what ever type of configuration you desire.

Below is a drawing of a larger building used in the commercial production of parakeets. The partition walls (walls separating the

Work area, sink and feed storage	8' x 10' Breeding Pen	8' x 10' Breeding Pen	8' x 10' Breeding Pen	8' x 10' Breeding Pen	8' x 10' Breeding Pen	8' x 10' Breeding Pen
4 foot wide hallway							
Holding Pen	8' x 10' Breeding Pen	8' x 10' Breeding Pen	8' x 10' Breeding Pen	8' x 10' Breeding Pen	8' x 10' Breeding Pen	8' x 10' Breeding Pen

individual pens) are covered with ½"x 1" welded wire. 1"x 4" pine boards are nailed on the wire covered partition walls and the nextboxes are hung on these. Each pen holds 40 pair of breeders.

Parakeet Nestboxes

Nestboxes can be purchased or built at home out of 3/8" plywood. Sizes vary, but a standard size is 6"x 8"x 8" deep, with a 1 ½" to 2" hole cut in it. Some of the store bought boxes have perches just under the hole, but these are not really necessary in colony breeding as the birds can zip in and out of the holes with ease without the perches. Parakeets do not build a nest, but some type of nesting material or litter is necessary to keep the eggs from rolling around inside the box. The boxes need to be cleaned between clutches and the litter or nesting material makes it a much easier process. Different people use different things. We used a course sawdust, since I had a source to get it free. I have known others to use ground corncobs, which is manufactured commercially as a bedding for small animals, or alfalfa pellets, or a mixture of the two.

It is not necessary for the boxes to be neatly lined up in a row, just hang them wherever space permits. However, the highest boxes should be hung no higher than eye level if your building design permits. That will allow for easy inspection without removing the box. All pens will need ample perch space for the birds. You can build perches out of ½" dowel rods or 2"x 2" or 1"x 2" planks. Either will work well.

Feeding and Watering Parakeets

Each pen will need its own feeding station as well as some type of watering system. There are a number of different types of automatic watering systems on the market that can be used, or you can use the old standby type that consist of a base drinking trough that screws onto a quart or gallon size jar. Either will work. If you use the drinking base that screws on to the jar, just be sure to change the water daily and wash not only the drinker base, but the inside of the jar as well. This is especially important during warm

Homemade box type feeders. The lower one is for the basic seed diet and the small one in the left side of the picture is used for the supplemental feed.

The greatest backyard business ever!

weather, since the inside of the bottle will often get a buildup of bacteria that can result in problems. The importance of clean drinking water is something that is often overlooked. Feeders can either be of the homemade type, or one of the poultry type feeders that will hold a week or more supply of feed.

What you feed your birds will determine to no small degree your success or failure in this business. Much scientific research has gone into the development of feeds that satisfy the nutritional requirements and needs of most all forms of domestic livestock. Unfortunately, there has not been a large degree of scientific research done on the nutritional requirements of parakeets. Although there are pelletized feeds on the market today that claim to offer a balanced diet for many types of birds, parakeets just don't seem to take to eating them as some of the other larger hookbills do. Therefore, the main staple of their diet continues to be seeds. Primarily three: proso millet, canary seed, and oat groats. To this, we add supplemental feed mixtures that help boost their protein as well as vitamin and mineral intake. In spite of the fact that we have no real scientific research on the nutritional requirements of parakeets, through the years many breeders have experimented with and came up with what appears to be some good feeding programs.

A good feeding program will consist of a free choice seed mixture being kept out at all times. Parakeets are by nature, nibblers, and it is very important that they never be without feed. Although parakeets feed the heaviest right after waking in the early morning and right before going to roost at dark, they will feed as many as 20 to 40 times throughout the day. Since their metabolism is so high and they burn energy so fast, a wise breeder will make sure his birds are never out of feed, even for a short period of time. That is extremely important if there are babies in the nestboxes.

A good seed mixture consists of 50% proso millet, 40% canary seed and 10% oat groats. The millet and canary seed ratio can be altered a little, depending on the price, but if you are producing lots of babies, they really need no less than 25% canary seed, as it is the softer of the two seeds and the adults really seem to prefer that over the millet when feeding large clutches of chicks. Over 10% oat groats is not recommended, as it will be too fattening and can lead to a number of problems. Although you can buy the individual seeds and mix your own, most feed companies make several different pre-mixed blends of parakeet feeds and these are much more convenient.

Parakeets husk the seed before eating it, eating only the inside kernel, therefore make sure you have feed in your feeder and not a feeder full of husk.

In addition to the seed mixture, there are many commercial feed mixture supplements on the market such as "Birds Choice", "Petamine", "Nutricare", etc. Some type of supplemental feeds such as these should be fed to insure that your birds get essential vitamins and minerals that are not in the seed mixture. There are many different brands of these supplements available; the above ones are just names that I happen to be familiar with. Additionally, some breeders will keep out a feed dish that will contain either turkey starter or wild game bird starter, just to add variety to the diet, although the birds generally will eat very little of those pelleted feeds.

Birds have no teeth with which to chew their food, therefore grit must be supplied to enable the birds gizzard to readily grind the seed to the consistency in which it can be easily digested. Commercial grits are available that are ground to the size suitable for parakeets.

Your birds will also need a mineral block in each breeding pen. These are commercially manufactured and will supply the bird with the calcium and phosphorus needed to make strong bones as well as eggshells. If laying birds are not supplied with the necessary calcium and phosphorus needed to produce the shells for the eggs as they are laid, it will be pulled it from their bones, which can result in birds with rickets. Not only will a lack of calcium and phosphorus in the diet affect the adult birds, but the newly hatched chicks can also have a calcium and phosphorus deficiency, resulting in splayed legs as well as other problems. Soft shelled eggs produced as a result of a calcium deficiency can also lead to egg binding in the hen, which can result in the loss of a valuable breeding hen. Mineral blocks also help the bird to keep its beak trimmed.

The feed you put into your birds will directly effect your results as a breeder. Before a baby chick becomes a baby chick, it is first an egg yoke. From the time the incubation process starts until the egg hatches, the embryo will get its nutrition from whatever the hen has incorporated into the egg yoke. Whatever she puts into the egg yoke will be determined by the feeding program you are using. Many times the least expensive feeding program will cost you in production losses, which, in turn, makes it a very expensive program. Don't shortchange yourself with a cheap feeding program.

Breeding Age Of Parakeets

Parakeets that are to be bred in colonies need to be around 6 months old before you hang the nestboxes in the flight pens. I have tried putting them to work at an earlier age, but it actually seemed to delay their laying. For reasons I cannot explain, the birds just don't seem to reach sexual maturity as early in a colony breeding operation as they do in cage breeding operations. Birds as young as 3 to 4 months old will often go to laying in a cage, but not so with colony breeding.

Determining The Age Of Parakeets

Distinguishing a baby parakeet from an adult one is not that difficult to do. But once the bird becomes an adult, it is much more difficult to tell whether the bird is one year old or four years old. That is one of the main reasons why you should only start with baby birds in this business.

The easiest way to tell a baby parakeet from an adult bird is by the bars or bands that go across the top of the birds head. On the normal colored birds, the bands will cross the neck and will continue the pattern of crossing the neck and head all the way down to the cere. As the chick ages, these bands will recede backwards. This is what is called "capping out". Usually the bird has capped out by the time it is 12 weeks old. As a general rule, by the time a bird has capped out you will be able to sex it with a very high degree of accuracy. A point worth noting is that the bird buyers mainly want baby birds. That is just the nature of the pet business. Babies are much easier to train, and will attach themselves to their owner much easier than will adult birds. After a parakeet has capped out, it's considered to be an adult and its value as a pet bird falls off dramatically.

Note the bands on the bird in the top of the picture are beginning to recede, indicating that it is an older bird than the one in the lower part of the photo. (approx.9 wks.)

6 week old bird with bands across forehead.

Albino, lutino and other color mutations will not have these bands, making it more difficult to tell the age of those types of birds. A secondary method of aging birds is the eyes. The color of a young birds eye is normally completely black, unless it is a pure albino or lutino, in which case the eye will be red. As the bird ages, a white ring appears around the outer part of the eye. As the bird gets older, the white ring will get wider, making the adult birds eye appear smaller than the baby birds eye.

The greatest backyard business ever!

In addition to capping out and the eyes, another means to help determine the age of birds is by checking their feet. Normally speaking, the claws of adult birds will be longer, or at least have a more weathered look to them.

Sexing Parakeets

Determining the sex of parakeets is really pretty easy, and unless you are color blind, you should be able to attain almost 100% accuracy with the normal colored parakeets. The mutations, or fancy colored ones are a little more difficult to sex, but even those can be sexed by an experienced person with around 95% accuracy. The little piece of meat just above the beak, where the nostrils are located is called a cere. When chicks first hatch, the cere will be a pinkish, or sometimes a bluish color. As the birds grow and mature, the cere on the male chicks will begin to turn more of a blue color, and the cere on the female chicks will begin to turn whitish, then a more tanish color, and finally a brown color. Some of the ceres will have a much more pronounced color than others, making it very easy to determine their sex. However, some of the color mutations, such as albino and lutino birds will not be quite as easy to determine their gender. Normally, in those birds, if the cere color is somewhere between a very light white to a dark brown, it will be a female. The cere of the males on the color mutations will be somewhere between a pink and bluish color. Sometimes the only part of the cere that has the determining color will be just around the nostrils, and the rest of the cere will be pink. Some birds can be sexed as early as 6 to 8 weeks of age, while others will need to be several months old. The color change of the cere from juvenile to adult bird is another way of determining the age of birds. **See color plate #1 on Page129.**

Putting Your Parakeets To Work

"Working birds" is a term that many bird breeders use when referring to the actual breeding and raising of their birds. I suppose that anyone who has ever raised a family will agree that the term fits, as work is definitely involved in raising a family.

We have determined that in colony breeding, your birds will need to be at least 6 months old. You need no more than 40 pair to a pen, depending, of course, on the size of your pen. Instead of one nestbox per pair, you should allow 20% more nestboxes than you actually need. This will give your birds a better selection and will help to cut back on the amount of squabbling that takes place when the birds are choosing their nesting boxes.

When pairing your birds up, it's a good idea to put a couple of extra males in the pen. Parakeets seem to pair up a little quicker with extra males, as it gives the females a bigger selection. The females are the most aggressive of the sexes, so never have more females in a pen than males. It will almost always lead to extreme fighting if there are not enough males to go around. Since these birds are territorial, you will never want to add any birds to a colony after they have started their breeding season. It creates havoc, and often results in fighting to the death, and it will invariably be one of your best female layers that will come out on the loosing end.

If your birds are in good condition, you will usually have eggs showing up in some of the boxes within a couple of weeks. Many birds such as turkey, quail, or chickens will lay an entire clutch of eggs before they start sitting and incubating the eggs, with the net result being that all the eggs hatch the same day. Not so with the parakeet.

The hen will lay an egg every other day, and will usually start setting and incubating the eggs after the first or second egg. Therefore, if she lays an egg every other day, and started incubating them after the second egg was laid, and she lays 6 eggs, they will hatch in the order they were laid. When the last chick hatches, the oldest one in the box will already be 12 days old. Many times if it is a very large clutch, the last chick to hatch will get trampled by its older siblings. Incubation time is approximately 18 days.

After the chicks begin to hatch, the feeding is shared by both parent birds. The male will go to the feeder and gorge himself, take it back to the nestbox and regurgitate the seed to the female who in turn feeds it to the baby chicks. The female produces a colostrum-like substance known as crop milk. She feeds this to the newly hatched chicks, with increasing amounts of partially digested seed. As the chicks grow older, the male begins to share in the feeding of the chicks by directly regurgitating the seed to the rapidly growing chicks. Baby parakeets grow incredibly fast and it is extremely important that they never be without feed, even for a few hours. By the time the chicks are 28 to 30 days old they are usually peeking out of the nestbox. Colony bred birds should be left to emerge from the nest on their own. That usually occurs when the chicks are around 30 to 35 days of age. The adult male continues to feed them for a few days after they leave the nestbox. Usually, after the chicks have been out of the nest for a few days, they can be taken out of the breeding pen and put into a holding pen until your next sale day.

Working Your Nestboxes

After your birds begin breeding, you will need to work out a schedule whereby you go through the building and check each nestbox a couple of times a week, making sure all is well within the box. It may sound like a lot of work, but it really doesn't take that much time, even if you have hundreds of pairs. Working the nestboxes will not disturb the birds, as they should be used to you by now. Gently raise the lid and take a look inside. You will be checking to see if the birds are using the box, whether or not you have eggs, eggs and chicks, or just chicks. If you are going to have problems with your birds, many times the nestbox is where they will show up first.

With young birds, the first clutch of eggs will sometimes be infertile and will need to be removed so the pair will start another clutch quickly. While this is not a common problem, it nevertheless needs to be covered. Incubation time for parakeets will vary a little, depending upon how tight the hen sits on the eggs, but will usually be around 18 days. If the eggs don't appear fertile after 12 to 14 days of incubation, they should be removed. During incubation, a fertile egg will become slightly darker than a fresh egg and will have an ever so slight bluish color to it, due to the developing embryo inside the shell. Infertile, or clear eggs as they are often called, will eventually turn a slightly yellowish color and become lighter in weight as the egg loses moisture and dries out. When the hen leaves the nestbox to go feed or get a drink, fertile eggs will retain heat much longer than will infertile eggs, provided they have been incubating for around 12 to 14 days, as the embryo itself is generating a degree of heat at that stage. In time, you will easily be able to distinguish fertile from infertile eggs.

Occasionally you will have adult female birds that are messy feeders and will plaster crop milk all over the face of the tiny chicks. This substance will harden like glue if left for a long period, and subsequent feedings will result in an ever increasing buildup on the chicks face, which, if not removed will result in a deformed beak rendering the bird somewhat worthless. It is easily removed if caught early, and is one of the reasons that frequent checking of the nestboxes is essential.

Another problem sometimes encountered when working nestboxes is a "wet nestbox". The normal droppings of baby parakeets are not overly loose and will usually dry very quickly. However, once in a while a pair of birds will have chicks that produce abnormal amounts of large, loose stools, resulting in a buildup of wet droppings within the nestbox. This can be caused by anything as simple as too much soft food in the diet, or too much of an intake of water in an extremely hot building, to something much more severe such as a bacterial infection. Many times these wet droppings will accumulate and harden on the feet and toes of the chicks in a wet nestbox. These hardened droppings can get as hard as concrete and will result in deformed feet or toes and should be removed before the buildup gets to that point.

Its not uncommon to lose a baby chick every now and then, and it is for that reason that the nestboxes need to be worked at least twice a week, removing any dead chick before it goes to deteriorating in the box. Since the chicks hatch in the order the eggs were laid, its common to have as much as two weeks or more difference in the ages of chicks. Often the last little chick to hatch will be trampled by the older chicks, resulting in the loss of the chick. Parakeets are good parents and don't mind feeding other baby chicks that have been fostered into their nestbox. If the clutch is quite large and there is a considerable amount of difference in the size of the chicks, you can take the smaller chick out of the nest and foster it out to another pair of birds that have chicks of similar size but fewer in numbers. If doing this, be sure and move the smaller chicks and not the larger ones. The larger chicks don't seem to transfer as well as the smaller ones. If chicks older than 3 weeks of age see the outside of a nest, they will often be inclined to start jumping out of the nest, and 3 weeks is too early for them to be leaving the nest.

Parakeets are prolific little birds, and many times by the time the last chick leaves the nest, the hen has already started laying another clutch of eggs. You will need to change the litter between clutches, but if the hen has already started laying again before you are able to do this, its not a problem. Working gently, raise the lid of the box, and if the hen doesn't leave on her own, gently work her out of the box. Work slowly, or she will scramble the new eggs. After she leaves the box, remove it and take the eggs out, dump the litter and replace with fresh, put the eggs back in and re-hang the nestbox. She will usually be back on the eggs within a few minutes.

Although it is your goal for all of your birds to be high layers, you will undoubtedly have some that are not as high of producers as you would like for them to be. These are the ones that you will want to use as foster parents if possible. That will take some of the load off of the higher producers. For instance, if you have a couple of pair of birds that have small clutches, you can combine the two clutches into one nest and the pair with the empty nest will usually start another clutch right away, helping to increase your production. Eggs can also be transferred as long as they are in approximately the same stage of the incubation process. For instance, you wouldn't want to transfer eggs that were ready to hatch into a nestbox with freshly laid eggs. Always use common sense.

Resting Your Birds

Although parakeets are quite prolific and will breed the year around, their production will usually start to fall off after they have been working continually for 6 to 9 months in colonies. It is a good idea to take the nest boxes down and give the birds a rest at that time. Generally speaking, the market for birds is slower in the hot summer months than at any other time of the year. If you rest your birds, time it so that your production will be the lowest during the months of June, July and August. It's not a good idea to completely shut your production down, but to have different groups of birds on a rotating system of working and resting.

Bird raisers use the term "breaking up" when referring to taking the nest boxes down and resting the birds. Breaking your birds up is a gradual process that takes a few weeks to complete. You don't just go in one day and take all the nestboxes down. When you decide its time to break your birds up, as you work your nestboxes, you simply start removing all fresh eggs. As the babies leave the nestboxes, pretty soon all the nestboxes in that colony will be empty if you have been removing the fresh eggs. At that time you can either remove the boxes or, if they don't have a perch on the front of them, you can simply turn the box around so the hole is on the backside next to the wall and the birds can't get inside. Just be sure that you remove or turn them all at once and not gradually, or there will be much fighting over the remaining nestboxes.

Normally a couple of month's rest is all that your birds will need. Then, you simply start the whole breeding process over again. By resting your birds, you will usually get 3 good years out of them before their production starts to fall off noticeably. Some breeders elect not to give their birds a rest at all, but to work them continually throughout the year and feel that they will take the needed rest on their own. You will probably want to try some of your birds both ways and form your own conclusion as to what works best for you, although I personally believe that the birds need the rest period.

Cage Breeding Parakeets

Earlier we discussed the advantages and disadvantages of both colony and cage breeding. If it is maximum income per square foot of building space that you desire, then cage breeding is the way to go. It does require more time, but the rewards are greater. As a rule of thumb, you can generally have twice as many birds in a building with a cage breeding setup than you can in the same building with a colony breeding setup. Since heating, cooling, and lighting expenses will be the same in either situation, you can see that the maximum income per square foot would be with the cages.

You can configure your cages to suit whatever size or shape of building that you have. Just remember to not hang the top row of cages too high, or you will need a stepladder to work your highest nestboxes. A small, short stool on rollers is a great asset when it comes to working the bottom rows of nestboxes if you have a very large setup. It will allow you to work the bottom row of cages while in a sitting position, rather than in a stooping or squatting position.

The Cage Breeding Unit

You can either purchase or build your own cages for cage breeding. If you elect to build them yourself, build them out of ½" by 1" welded wire and make sure to grind the sharp burrs off of the door and feeder openings that you cut in the cages. Those burrs will scratch your hands raw over a period of time if you don't grind them smooth. Everybody has their own idea as to what is the best size cage to use. Some breeders use a 12" x 12" by 18" long cage, while others use a 12" x 12" x 15" cage. I personally like and recommend the larger size cages. Cages can be constructed so that one feeder will service two compartments, or two pair of birds as you will see in some of the pictures in this chapter. This will help to cut down on the cost of the feeders, as well as it speeds up the feeding process. Each cage will need a drinker of some description, either manual or automatic. I strongly recommend the automatic watering system if you have very many pairs of birds. They are not that expensive and they are enormous time savers. Each cage will also need some type of tray or catch pan underneath that will catch the seed husk as well as the bird droppings. A perch inside each cage is required. Nestboxes are the same size as colony breeding nestboxes. In colony breeding, it made no difference whether or not the nestbox had a perch on it, but most cage breeders prefer to have a perch on the nestbox, since perch space within the cage is limited.

The greatest backyard business ever!

Several excellent cage breeding setups.

These cages are home made. Note how the trays are designed to catch the seed husk and droppings and can be easily cleaned, either by dumping the contents or with a shop vacuum.

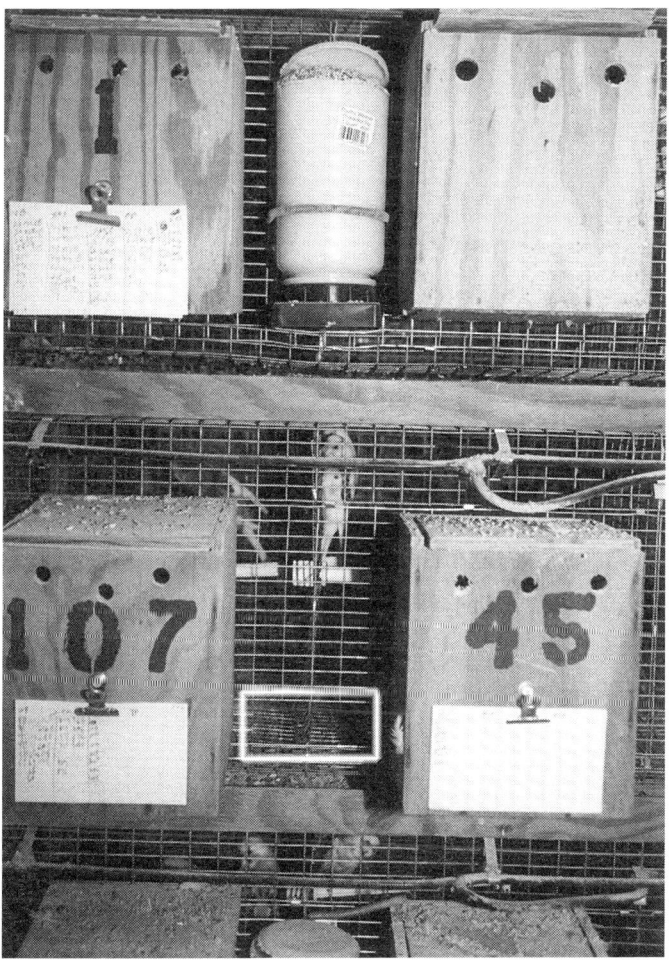

The feeder is removed between the middle nestboxes in this set of cages to show how one feeder will service two cages, thus reducing the time to feed. The partition between the two cages is simply notched out to allow half of the feeder to be in each cage. This cage breeding setup is also equipped with an automatic water system, making it a very efficient operation.

The greatest backyard business ever!

Feeding

Although the diet is the same with cage breeding as it is with colony breeding, the method of feeding is a little different. With colony breeding, each pen had a feeding station and the seed, grit, and supplement were fed in three separate containers. In cage breeding, the separate items are usually mixed together and put into the same feeder, since space limits the amount of feeders that you will have in a cage. Below are a couple of mixing formulas that have proven successful with a number of breeders. The cans mentioned are 1# coffee cans.

Formula #1
50# of parakeet mix
½ can parakeet grit
3 cans game bird starter
½ can vitamin mineral supplement such as Birds Choice or Petamine
Mix well

Formula #2
50# parakeet mix
½ cup wheat germ oil
½ can parakeet grit
½ can vitamin mineral supplement such as Birds Choice or Petamine
3 cans turkey starter
Mix well

There are a number of different vitamin/mineral supplements on the market and you will most likely use whatever brand you can get locally. The addition of turkey or game bird starter to the diet is a way of boosting not only the protein needed for growing chicks, but also the vitamins and minerals as well as other trace elements that have been formulated specifically for fowl, although most birds will eat only very small amounts of it.

While some breeders mix everything together and put it in one feeder, others prefer to put the seed in one feeder and the supplemental feed and grit in a separate little feeder, claiming the birds waste less feed that way. It all boils down to your own personal choice, but I am a big fan of simplicity.

Small mineral blocks are also attached to the inside of each cage for their daily calcium and phosphorus needs.

Breeding Age Of Birds In Cages

Parakeets will go to work at a much earlier age in cages than in colonies, probably because there are less birds to distract one another during the bonding and mating process. While some breeders will hold their birds until they are 5 to 6 months old, many breeders will put the birds to work by the time they are only 3 or 4 months old. It's not unheard of for birds that are 4 to 5 months old to already be hatching chicks of their own.

Putting Your Birds To Work In Cages

Putting your birds to work in cages is quite a bit different than in colonies. You have much more control over your production with cage breeding and will probably pair your birds up according to what colors you want to produce. You will simply put the male and female together in the breeding cage and hang the nestbox. In colony breeding, you must hang all the nestboxes in a pen at the same time to prevent fighting over nesting sites, where with cage breeding, its not necessary to put large groups to work at the same time.

Provided the pair get along together and bond, all is well. However, sometimes it doesn't work out exactly like that. In the event the pair are not compatible, some serious fighting can take place, sometimes even to the point that one bird will kill the other. If that happens, it is usually the male that comes out on the short end of things. In the event that some fighting does take place, its best to go ahead and re-mate the pair as quickly as possible. Since parakeets are territorial, in all likelihood the aggressor has already claimed the cage as its territory and may fight another bird that you may try to re-mate it with in that same cage, so it's best to move the aggressive bird to another cage, thus removing it from its territory and starting out afresh. Sometimes this mating process can be frustrating, and I have had some females that I just couldn't find a mate for. Sell those and don't waste your time.

Working Your Nestboxes In Cage Breeding

Working your nestboxes with cages is basically just like it is in colony breeding, with a couple of exceptions. Most breeders will remove the baby chicks just as they are ready to emerge from the nestbox, whereas in colony breeding you let them emerge from the nest on their own. For some reason, once in a while the adults will kill the babies if they come out of the nestbox and are allowed to remain in the breeding cage. Therefore, the safe thing to do is to remove the baby just as it gets old enough to come out of the nestbox on its own. Since you need to be working your boxes twice a week anyway, that's not hard to do. Learning when to pull your babies out of the box is not at all difficult, and you will soon be able to tell within a day or so of when they will come out on their own. As a

Five chicks that are almost ready to leave the nestbox. The underside of the wing needs to be fully feathered before removing the chick from the nest.

This chick will be ready to come out of the box in about another week.

good rule of thumb, if the bird is fully feathered under the wing, it is ready to come out. After you take them out, you will need to put them in a holding cage, not a flight pen, but a cage that has grain scattered on the floor. Many breeders will keep an adult male in the holding cage, since he will usually feed the babies if they go to begging to be fed, as they sometimes will.

Many breeders will keep an adult male in the holding cage with the babies, since he will usually feed the young weanlings if they go to begging to be fed, as they sometimes will. Note that the bottom of this holding cage is completely covered with feed, thus assuring that the baby birds will have no trouble finding feed while they are beginning to eat on their own.

This group of babies are ready for market.

Another nice thing about cage breeding is that you will be able to keep an accurate production record of each pair. If some birds are not producing like you feel they should be, you can get rid of them, whereas in colony breeding, it is next to impossible to know who is doing what. These records will help you to determine which birds are your top producers, and it is from those that you will want to save offspring from for your replacement breeders.

Resting Your Birds In Cage Breeding

As a general rule, most commercial breeders who use the cage breeding method do not rest their birds, but work them straight through until their production goes to falling off. Some clutches will be larger, some smaller, and sometimes they may take a brief rest on their own. By keeping accurate records on an index card attached to each nestbox, you will be able to tell when the production falls off and stays off. That is the time to replace them. If you decide to rest your birds in cages, you break them up in the same manner as you do with colony breeding.

Chapter 10

Breeding Cockatiels

Breeding Cockatiels In Colonies

Although cockatiels breed well in cages, there seems to be a larger percentage of breeders who prefer to breed them in colonies. Cockatiels have a good disposition and will mix well with other birds in the same building. In fact, they will even tolerate other birds nesting in the same pen with them, provided the other birds are of a non-aggressive nature. I have had a few pair of finches or doves in the same pens with cockatiels and they did just fine. However, most breeders elect not to mix the species in the same pen.

An 8'x 10' pen is an ideal size and will accommodate from 8 to 10 pair of birds. A good rule of thumb is to allow 5 square feet of floor space per bird. Some breeders will crowd them a bit more than that, however I have found that over 10 pair in a pen this size will normally result in less production per pair within the pen and not more, because of quarreling among themselves. Cockatiels have strong beaks and I recommend ½"x1" welded wire or ½" x ½" hardware cloth for the construction of your pens.

Notice how the cockatiels have chewed the outer layer off of the interior wall in this aviary. There is no danger here, though, since this is ½ inch plywood.

Cockatiel Nestboxes

Nestboxes can be either purchased or you can build them at home yourself. If you build them yourself, use ½" plywood and they will last longer, since cockatiels can be pretty destructive, especially in colony breeding setups. Dimensions can vary, but a 12"x12"x12" is a good size, although some people prefer a smaller, deeper box such as 9"x 9" x 15". Regardless of the size, cut a 3" hole in the front about 2" from the top. An 8"x 3" strip of the welded wire stapled to the inside of the box just under the hole acts as a ladder and makes it easier for the birds to get out of the deeper box. Many cockatiel breeders prefer to put a perch on the front of the box about an inch below the hole, but it really doesn't seem to make much of a difference to the birds whether or not the box has a perch, as they can go in and out with ease in either case. A couple of ½' holes drilled in the sides towards the top will allow for a little better ventilation inside.

Although cockatiels do not build a nest, you will still have to put some type of litter or nesting material in the bottom of the box. It not only keeps the eggs from rolling around, but will aid greatly when it comes to cleaning the nestbox between clutches. Course sawdust, wood shavings or ground corncobs make a good litter and are all commercially available. Some breeders like to use a mixture of ground corncobs and alfalfa pellets as a nesting material. It makes no difference in what order or fashion you hang your nestboxes in the breeding pens, just as long as you don't hang the boxes so high that you will need to remove them when it comes time for inspection.

You will need to provide ample perch space in each pen. Perches can be built out of ½" dowel rods or 1"x 2" or 2"x 2" planks.

Feeding and Watering Cockatiels

Each pen of birds will need its own feeding station as well as some type of watering system. I truly like the automatic water systems that are on the market today. They are much better than the ones years ago that had a lot of problems with the individual drinkers dripping. Automatic water systems are definitely time

A cockatiel feeding station with home style feeders.

savers if you have very many pens of birds, and you will consider their cost as money well spent. But if you don't have a lot of birds, the poultry drinking base that screws on a jar and is inverted works great. Just be sure to do a good job of washing not only the drinker base itself, but also the inside of the jar, as bacteria will often buildup and cause a scum to start growing inside of the jar that can create some major problems with your birds. Please remember to not overlook the importance of a clean supply of drinking water; many breeders do. Your feeders can be of the homemade type or you can purchase the poultry type feeders that have a hopper that will hold a week or more supply of feed.

Your feeding program will directly effect the degree of success or failure that you will experience in breeding cockatiels. What you get out of your birds will be no better than what you put in them. There has not been a lot of scientific research conducted on pet birds, at least not to the degree that there has been with the game bird and poultry industries. While there are pelleted feeds on the market that are no doubt good for the birds, most cockatiels don't readily adapt to eating them, and many are simply cost prohibitive to feed to anything other than a house pet.

Game bird feed, which is economical in price, is a balanced feed formulated on the known nutritional needs of a game bird, which I believe would closely resemble the nutritional needs of a cockatiel, if those were truly known. However, cockatiels just don't seem to adapt to eating these pelleted diets very well. Additionally, most of the pelleted feeds seem to cause the birds to have a much looser, bulkier stool than normal, which results in wet, messy nestboxes, creating a whole new list of problems. Practically all large commercial cockatiel breeders still feed a diet that is basically seed, and supplement it with various things in an attempt to balance the diet.

The cockatiel diet consist mainly of a mixture of several different types of seeds, including millet, canary seed, oat groats and sunflower or safflower seed. Cockatiels will do well on a seed mixture that is the same basic mixture recommend for parakeets which consist of

50% white proso millet, 40% canary seed and 10% oat groats. You can provide sunflower or safflower in a separate container. Although safflower is suppose to be a higher quality seed than sunflower, we could not tell a difference and the birds seem to take to the sunflower much better. In addition to the basic seed diet, you will need to feed one of the commercial feed mixture supplements that are on the market such as "Birds Choice", "Petamine", "Nutricare", etc. These will help ensure that your birds get the essential vitamins, minerals and other trace elements that are lacking in a straight seed diet. Many breeders will also keep a separate dish of game bird starter or turkey starter in each pen, even though the birds will only eat small quantities of this type of feed..

Most of the feed companies that cater to bird breeders will have a cockatiel blend or mix that has all of the above ingredients already premixed into it. These are convenient and work fine, as long as it is a well balanced blend of seed and not loaded up with the cheaper millets. In addition to the seed diet and vitamin/mineral supplement, most breeders will give some type of fresh fruit or vegetable to their birds daily, especially when baby chicks are in the nestboxes. Fresh corn or shredded carrots are the most commonly used, putting out only the amount that the birds will clean up within an hour or so. Cracked or whole kernel corn, such as is fed to other types of livestock, can be boiled and fed in the place of fresh corn or vegetables. It's inexpensive and the birds love it. If you feed these soft supplemental feeds, be sure that you do it at approximately the same time every day, as the birds will learn to wait on it to feed to their babies.

I know of some cockatiel breeders who will mix about a half of a cup of wheat germ oil to 50 pounds of feed. This is thought to help increase breeding as well as fertility, since wheat germ oil is an excellent source of vitamin E. However, since the birds husk the seed, it seems to me that most of the wheat germ oil is lost during the husking process. I believe adding the wheat germ oil to the fresh vegetables is a much better avenue of getting it into the birds. Just be careful and don't add too much, thinking if a little is good, a lot is better, as that is not the case. Too much will invariably cause digestive problems.

Cockatiels have no teeth with which to chew their food, and grit must be supplied to enable the gizzard to grind the seed to a consistency in which digestion can readily take place. Commercial grit made from either ground up oyster shell or granite is available in the size that cockatiels will readily accept. Cockatiels, like parakeets, husk their seed, eating only the inside of the seed kernel. That being the case, make sure you have feed in your feeders and not a feeder full of husk. That may sound elementary to you, but I have actually known newcomers to the business practically starve their birds by mistaking the husk for seed.

Your cockatiels will also need a mineral block in each breeding pen. Mineral blocks will supply the birds with the necessary calcium and phosphorus needed to make their eggshells while keeping their bones strong. If laying birds are not supplied with the necessary calcium and phosphorus needed to produce the shells for the eggs as they are laid, it will be pulled it from their bones, which can result in birds with rickets. Not only will a lack of calcium and phosphorus in the diet affect the adult birds, but the newly hatched chicks can also have a calcium and phosphorus deficiency, resulting in splayed legs as well as other problems. Soft shelled eggs produced as a result of a calcium deficiency can also lead to egg binding in the hen, which can result in the loss of a valuable breeding hen. The mineral blocks also aid in keeping their beak trimmed.

Captive bred cockatiels are nibblers by nature and will feed throughout the day, although the heaviest feeding will be at the beginning and ending of their day. It is extremely important that your birds have feed available to them at all times, especially when young chicks are in the nest. Never let your feeders run dry.

Breeding Age Of Cockatiels

Cockatiels will often begin breeding at arouind 6 to 8 months of age, although its not uncommon for the first clutch of eggs to be infertile if they are allowed to breed at that early age. In my opinion, 9 to 10 months is a better age in which to begin breeding cockatiels. As is the case with parakeets, cockatiels seem to begin breeding quicker and at an earlier age if in being bred in cages rather than in colonies.

Sexing Your Cockatiels

Cockatiels are very difficult to sex until after they have gone through their first molt and shed their juvenile feathers. That usually occurs at around 5 to 6 months of age, and after that most of them are not that difficult to sex, but until then, as a general rule the young juvenile birds will have the same coloration of adult female birds. After their first molt the coloration will be as follows:

- **Normal female cockatiel:** basic gray color with light orange colored cheek patch. Bars on underside of primary wing and tail feathers.
- **Normal male cockatiel:** basic gray color with a bright yellow head and bright orange cheek patch. Absence of bars on underside of primary wing and tail feathers after molt.
- **Female pearly cockatiel**: has the pearly, lacy yellow colored feathers on back and wing feathers. Bars under wing.
- **Male pearly cockatiel:** after the molt, looks just like a normal male cockatiel, but will still carry the pearly gene.
- **Pied female cockatiel:** gray and white spotted. Usually there will be some bars on the underside of the primary wing and tail feathers, although sometimes these are very faint and hard to see.
- **Pied male cockatiel:** gray and white spotted with solid colored primary wing and tail feathers. Head will usually be more yellow colored than females and the cheek patch will be brighter.
- **Lutino female cockatiel:** although they are sometimes very hard to see, the females will retain the yellow bars on the underside of the primary wing and tail feathers that they had as juveniles.
- **Lutino male cockatiel:** There will be no bars on the underside of the primary wing and tail feathers. A lutino cockatiel is often referred to an albino cockatiel.

There are a number of different color varieties such as cinnamon, fallow, pearly pied, etc., but the sexing principal is somewhat the same. Females will usually have bars on the underside of the primary wing and tail feathers whereby males will lack these. And males will always have brighter colored faces and cheek patches. **See Color Plate #2. Page 129**

Sexing birds by their coloration is reliable only after they have went through their first molt and shed their juvenile feathers, which is usually at around 6 months of age. This sexing process can be sped up considerably by plucking one of the primary wing feathers or tail feathers of a bird as young as 3 months old, as long as the feather is in the fully hardened stage and has quit growing. If the feather has no blood in it and is fully hard, it's safe to pluck. Counting from the end of the wing, pluck the 5th or 6th primary wing feather by giving it a quick, sharp pull. Within about a month, a new feather will have grown out enough to see whether or not it has retained the yellow bars. If it did, it's a female, if not, it's a male.

A secondary way in which to sex cockatiels is by feeling the pelvis bone. The pelvic bones are a little wider apart in the female

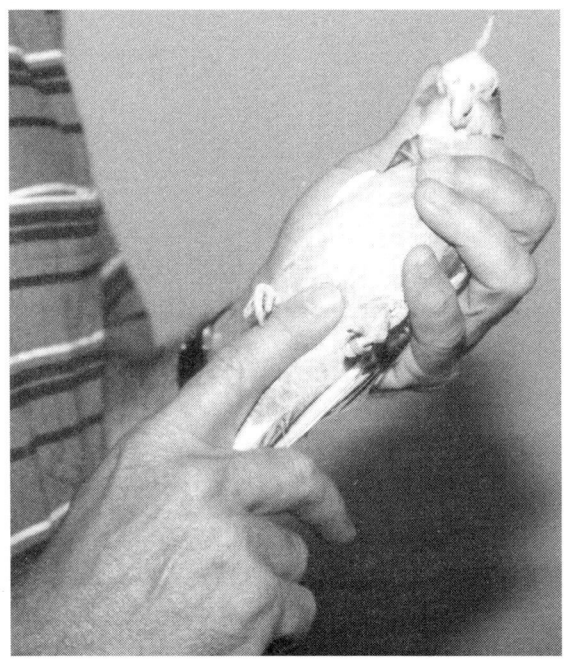

When sexing cockatiels with the pelvic method, hold the bird as pictured. Place your index finger on the bird's breast and gently slide it down the breastbone towards the vent. You will feel two tiny bones right at the vent. The bones will almost be touching if it is a male, while the female's bones will be wider apart.

than in the male, but this can be tricky if the bird has not yet laid an egg, although it is usually pretty reliable.

One other characteristic of cockatiels is that the males are usually much more vocal and whistle more than the females.

Determining The Age Of Cockatiels

This can be tricky with cockatiels. While young birds are often a little more slender than adult birds, that's not always the case. I have seen some baby cockatiels that were hatched from very large breed stock that were just as large as the adult birds that were of a smaller stock. However, the crest of younger birds will be smaller than the crest on mature birds, and the toe nails of adults will usually be longer, as well as the feet will usually have a more worn, rugged look than those of the younger birds. The same can be said of the beak of the adult birds. It will have a more worn, rugged look if the bird is very old.

The coloration of the beak is another way to tell young cockatiels from the adults. Baby birds will have a pinkish colored beak that will gradually turn a darker color and then usually a grayish color by the time they are 5 to 6 months old. It is extremely difficult to tell the age of cockatiels once they have reached sexual maturity. Birds that are 10 years old can easily be mistaken for birds that are one year old. Therefore, when starting out in this business the, the only true way of knowing the age of your birds is to start with youngsters.

Putting Your Cockatiels To Work

Once your birds have reached proper breeding age, you will no doubt be eager to allow them to start breeding and raising baby chicks for you to market. After your birds have reached breeding age, determine the amount of pairs your pen will hold using the formula of 5 square feet of floor space per bird, remembering not to make your pens too large. Less than 10 pair per pen is ideal. If possible, when pairing your birds up, allow a couple of extra males in each pen so as to give the females a better selection of mates. This will sometimes speed up the pairing and bonding process. Just remember, never have extra females in a pen as this will usually result in disruptive behavior that will interfere with the bonding and breeding process, as the females are the more aggressive of the sexes. Overall, cockatiels are not considered to be an aggressive bird and have a very good disposition, with serious fighting being quite rare.

It's a good idea to hang about 50% more nestboxes in each breeding pen than the birds actually need. A pen with 8 pair of birds should have at least a dozen nestboxes in it. This gives your birds plenty of nesting choices and will usually speed up the selection of a nesting site, thus speeding up the breeding process. Be sure and hang all of the boxes that you intend to hang in the pen at the same time. Adding boxes at a later date can create problems, as will adding additional birds.

Cockatiels are an easy bird to breed. Assuming that you have had your birds on a good nutritional program, that they are of the proper age and you are providing an environment suitable to breeding, they should start pairing up within a week or so. Your first eggs can appear within two weeks. Once your birds have completely paired up, it's a good idea to remove any extra males you may have put in the pen. The whole purpose of the extra males was to give the females a choice, thus speeding up the mating process. Once they've made that choice, you can get the extras out. This just takes a little time, but it can easily be done over the course of a few weeks.

One positive thing about cockatiels vs. parakeets, lovebirds or finches is the fact that you won't have a lot of pairs in each pen. You can usually stand and observe a pen of cockatiels and see which ones are going in and out of the nestboxes. With cockatiels, both male and female will incubate the eggs, and very often both birds will be in the nestbox at the same time. On a daily basis, check each nestbox by gently raising the lid and looking inside. Nesting cockatiels are usually pretty docile, especially if they are accustomed to you being in the pen with them.

Once you have an egg in the nest and you find a bird inside, take a magic marker or marks-a-lot pen and put a mark on the white patch on the birds wing. If you are very gentle and don't make fast moves, the birds will usually just keep sitting on the eggs, although occasionally they will move over to one corner of the nestbox or even leave the box, but as soon as you are out of there, they will be right back in the box. Since you don't have a lot of pairs in each pen, you can color code the pairs. For instance, once you put a red mark on a female in one particular nestbox, sooner or later you will catch the male inside the same nest and put a red mark on him. That will be your pair. Color-code the next pair black, blue, orange, etc. The marker ink will usually stay on the feathers for six to eight weeks and you will soon be able to tell which birds are working and which ones are not.

If after a couple of months you have birds without any marks on them, meaning that you have not caught them inside a nestbox, you can remove them and try re-pairing them in another pen. The object is to get all the birds paired up with a compatible mate and then leave them together from then on. Cockatiels will produce for many, many years, and this initial pairing process is a one time thing, so work at trying to get each and every bird paired up. Once done, leave them alone.

Once she begins laying, the female cockatiel will lay an egg every other day until she lays her entire clutch, which is usually around 4 to 6 eggs, although 7 to 8 are not uncommon. Cockatiels will normally start incubating their eggs after the second egg is laid, and the eggs will hatch in the order they were laid. Therefore, the chicks will hatch on an every other day schedule just as the eggs were laid, resulting in the last chick to hatch sometimes being as much as two weeks younger than its older sibling. That age difference in the chicks can cause the last little chick to hatch to be trampled by its nest mates, especially if it is a large clutch. Incubation time is approximately 21 days.

Both birds share in the incubation of the eggs as well as the feeding of the newly hatched young. As the first chicks begin to hatch, the hen will hardly leave the nest at all. The feeding starts with the male, who will gorge himself at the feeder, take it back to the nestbox and regurgitate the feed to the female, who in turn feeds it to the newly hatched chicks. The female also produces a colostrum-like

substance known as crop milk, which she feeds to the youngest chicks. As the baby chicks grow, she increases the amount of partially digested seed that she feeds them. Eventually, they are old enough that the male will bypass the hen, feeding the baby chicks directly himself.

The importance of a nutritious diet cannot be overstated, as baby cockatiels grow incredibly fast, and by the time they are five weeks old they will begin leaving the nestbox. Cockatiels do not wean as quickly as other birds, and care must be taken not to take the young birds out of the breeding pen at too early of an age. The male will usually continue to feed the chicks for a week or so after they have left the nest. It's a good idea to leave them in the breeding pen with their parents until they are 8 to 9 weeks of age to assure that they are feeding adequately on their own.

Working Your Nestboxes

Once you have put the birds to work, you will need to make yourself a schedule whereby you go through your building and check each nestbox at least twice a week. Working the nestboxes will not disturb the birds, as by now they should be familiar with you. If your nestboxes are hung no higher than eye level, removing them for inspection is not necessary nor is it advised. Gently raise the lid and take a look inside. You will be checking to see if the birds are using the box, whether or not you have eggs or nestlings, and in general what's going on with your birds. Usually, if you are going to have a problem with your birds, the nestbox will be the first place it will show up.

With young cockatiels, the first clutch of eggs will occasionally be infertile and will need to be removed so the pair will start another clutch as quick as possible. Incubation time for cockatiels will vary a little, depending upon how tight the hen sits on the eggs, but will usually be around 21 days. If the eggs don't appear fertile after 14 to 16 days of incubation, they should be removed. During incubation, a fertile egg will become slightly darker than a fresh egg and will have an ever so slight bluish color to it, due to the developing embryo inside the shell. Infertile, or clear eggs as they are sometimes called, will eventually turn a slightly yellowish color and become lighter in weight as the egg loses moisture and dries out. When the hen leaves the nestbox to go feed or get a drink, fertile eggs will retain heat much longer than will infertile eggs, provided they have been incubating for around 14 to 16 days, as the embryo itself is generating a degree of heat at that stage. In time, you will easily be able to distinguish fertile from infertile eggs.

Occasionally you will have birds that are messy feeders and will plaster crop milk all over the face of the tiny chicks. This substance will harden like glue if left for a long period, and subsequent feedings will result in an ever increasing buildup on the chicks face, which, if not removed will result in a deformed beak rendering the bird somewhat worthless. It is easily removed if caught early, and is one of the reason that frequent checking of the nestboxes is essential.

Another problem sometimes encountered when working nestboxes is a "wet nestbox". The normal droppings of cockatiels are not overly loose and will usually dry rather quickly. However, once in a while a pair of birds will have chicks that produce abnormal amounts of large, loose stools, resulting in a buildup within the nestbox of wet droppings. These abnormal droppings can be caused by anything as simple as too much soft food in the diet, or an intake of too much water(which can happen if your building gets too hot), to something much more severe such as a bacterial infection. Many times the chicks in a wet nestbox will have the droppings accumulate and harden on their feet. These hardened droppings can get as hard as plaster and will result in deformed feet or toes and should be removed before the buildup gets to that point.

Once in a while you will lose a baby chick and that's just another reason that it is so important to work your nestboxes at least twice a week, removing any dead nestling before it starts to decompose in the box. Since the chicks hatch in the order that the eggs were laid, you will have chicks of various ages in the same nestbox, often as much as 10 to 14 days difference in age from the oldest to the youngest. Cockatiels grow extremely fast, and although I have never weighed one, I would estimate that a 14 day old cockatiel can weigh as much as 20 or more times the weight of a tiny chick that has just hatched. You can easily see that if there are five or six nestlings in a nestbox that are on up around 10 to 18 days old, and a late hatch chick comes along, his chances of getting trampled and smashed are pretty good. These last little chicks are the ones that will occasionally not make it. Honestly, it amazes me how that any of the last little chicks in a large clutch are able survive, but nature is an amazing thing. The parent birds will somehow hear the crying chick even though it is completely covered by a pile of older siblings, and manage to feed it the crop milk that is reserved for the youngest hatchlings, while feeding the older chicks a completely different diet. Incredible.

Cockatiels make good parents and normally raise their young very well on their own. Some will raise much larger clutches than others, and cockatiels will accept baby chicks from other pairs. When fostering chicks out to other pairs, it is best to always foster the smallest chicks. If a pair has an extremely large clutch, say 6 to 8 chicks, you can take the youngest chick or two and put them in with a smaller clutch of chicks that are approximately the same age. This helps to even up the workload a bit, and is a way in which you can increase your production somewhat, as the pair that had the larger clutch will have an empty nest a little sooner and will usually start back laying a little quicker. Actually, you can even foster eggs that are getting ready to hatch if you fear the newly hatched chick will be trampled. Just try to foster the eggs in with other eggs that you feel are in about the same stage of incubation.

When fostering chicks, always foster the youngest chicks, since the larger ones don't seem to transfer as well as the smaller ones. If chicks are older than around 3 to 4 weeks old and they see the outside of a nest, often they will start trying to jump out of the nest and leave it prematurely. If you must transfer an older chick, cover its eyes with your hand so that it will not be able to see the outside of the box and most of the time that will work.

Good quality cockatiels that are well fed and have a good breeding environment are rather prolific and its not uncommon for the pair to begin laying a new clutch of eggs before the last chick leaves the nestbox. The litter will need to be changed between clutches, but if the hen has already started laying by the time the last chick leaves the box, it's not a problem. Simply ease the lid off the nestbox and if the birds don't come out on their own, gently work them out of the box, being careful not to excite them, lest they scramble the new eggs. Once the birds leave the box, remove it and take the fresh eggs out, dump the litter and replace with fresh, put the eggs back in and re-hang the nextbox. The birds will usually be back on the eggs within a very short time.

Once the baby cockatiels begin to leave the nestbox, it's difficult for many people to tell the youngsters from the adults, because they are often just about as large. And since baby cockatiels need to remain in the breeding pen with the adults for a couple of weeks after they leave the nestbox, it can then become even harder to distinguish them from the older birds. Of course it's very easy to tell a mature normal male cockatiel from the youngsters because of his bright yellow head, but it's not quite that easy with the pieds, albinos or even the normal gray females.

About a week before the nestlings are due to start coming out of the nest, many breeders will take a felt tip marker or lipstick and put a small mark on one wing of the youngster while working their nestboxes. This mark will stay on the wing for about 6 weeks and will make it much easier to spot the youngsters after they leave the nest. Just be sure and not mark them too heavily or it can have an effect on selling them. As a buyer, I have had breeders to bring baby cockatiels in that were so heavily marked with lipstick or red markers, that they almost resembled a flamingo in color. Youngsters will also have smaller feet and lighter colored beaks as a general rule.

Banding the adult birds before the breeding season begins is the easiest way that you can distinguish the adults from the youngsters. By using numbered legbands, you can also keep accurate records on the adult birds, such as their age and who their mate is.

Ever so often, usually once every couple of weeks, you will want to catch the young birds that you feel are old enough to remove from the breeding pen and put them in a holding pen where you will keep them until they are ready to market. You will want to keep a record on each pen telling how many babies you took out and the dates, so at the end of their breeding cycle you will have a good production record of that pen. Because cockatiel nestboxes are so large, you can write individual breeding records on the front of each box and you will be able to tell what each pair did that season, provided they don't change boxes, which they sometimes will do.

Resting Your Birds

Cockatiels are a prolific bird and will breed 12 months out of the year, although after 3 to 4 clutches their production will begin to fall off and they will produce smaller clutches. Usually the quality of the chicks will also begin to decline noticeably. This is especially true with colony bred birds. It's a good idea to give the birds a rest at that time. As a general rule the market for pet birds is much slower during the summer months than at any other time of the year, which will usually result in summer prices being the lowest prices of the year. If you rest your birds, you should time it so that the months of June, July and August will be your lowest production months, and plan to be back in full production by October, as the demand is usually picking back up by then. I don't believe it is a good idea to ever have all of your birds completely shut down, but to have them on a rotating basis of some working while others are resting.

Bird raisers use the term "breaking up" when referring to taking the nestboxes down and giving their birds a rest. It is a gradual process that will take a few weeks to complete. Once you decide its time to break a pen of birds up, as you work the nestboxes in that pen, you will need to start removing all the freshly laid eggs. Over the course of a couple of weeks your nestboxes will become empty as the nestlings mature and leave the box. At that time you can either cover the holes of the nestboxes by turning them around and hanging them backwards, or remove them from the pen. Which ever you do, the hens will stop laying once they no longer have a place in which to nest.

A six to eight week rest will usually be sufficient time for the birds to rest and replenish themselves and after that, you just start the whole process over again. However, the second time around it's much easier as the birds are already paired and mated. By resting your cockatiels, you will extend their breeding life considerably. Cockatiels can reproduce quite well for around 8 to 10 years. After that, their production goes to falling off noticeably and it's best to have already saved back some replacement breeders for birds that reach that age.

There are some breeders who do not like to rest their birds at all, preferring instead to work them 12 months out of the year, theorizing that the birds will take a rest on their own when they need it. I don't necessarily subscribe to that theory, or at least not with colony breeding of cockatiels, and besides, if they are going to produce only a certain amount of offspring per year, I like to have the control over what months that offspring will be produced in, so as to sell at the highest possible prices.

Cage Breeding Cockatiels

The same advantages and disadvantages of cage breeding vs. colony breeding apply to cockatiel breeding as they did with parakeet breeding mentioned earlier in this book. You can definitely put more birds in a given area with cage breeding than you can with colony breeding, as well as you will have much more control over the colors that you will produce.

The Cage Breeding Unit

As was the case with parakeets, you can either purchase or build your own cages for breeding cockatiels. If you build them

Cockatiel cages come in a variety of sizes. If you build your own, just make sure that they are large enough.

Raising Pet Birds For Profit

yourself, I recommend using ½" x 1" welded wire, making sure to grind smooth all sharp burrs from around the openings that you cut in the cages for the doors and feeders. I believe a minimum cage size for a pair of cockatiels is 18" deep by 18" tall by 30" long. Each cage will need some type of tray or catch pan underneath it that will catch the seed husk as well as the bird droppings. Many feed stores or aviary supply companies carry cages that are approximately that size or a little larger that work great for breeding cockatiels. Most are stackable and also include a metal tray for catching the droppings and seed husk. A cage this size needs a perch at both ends with ½' dowel rods being the choice material for perches. If you plan to have a considerable amount of cages, a low pressure automatic watering system sure will cut back on the amount of time it will take to care for your birds. Nestboxes are the same with cages as with colonies, and you will hang them from the outside of the cage rather than on the inside.

Feeding

The feeding program will be basically the same with cages as it was with colonies, with one exception. I do not recommended that you provide free choice sunflower or safflower. Feed the mix that has it already included. Cockatiels bred in cages do not get the same amount of exercise as those that are bred in colonies. Sunflower and safflower are very high in oil and if fed free choice, some of the birds will no doubt become overly fat as a result of overeating the high fat content seed. Birds that are too fat will not reproduce well and your production will suffer as a result. In addition to your seed mixture, you will need to provide the same type of vitamin-mineral supplements as mentioned earlier in colony breeding as well as each cage will need its own mineral block for egg production.

Breeding Age Of Cockatiels In Cages

Cockatiels seem to start laying a little earlier in cages than in colonies. I'm not exactly sure why that is, other than the fact that if they are confined together in a cage there is less distractions and they will settle down and go to nesting at a somewhat earlier age. But it's still a good idea not to allow them to breed until they are 7 or 8 months old.

Putting Your Birds To Work In Cages

Putting the birds to work in cages is different than in colonies. You will have more control over the colors that are produced, so you will want to pair them accordingly. Cockatiels are not nearly as aggressive as many other birds and will usually not fight to the extent that they injure themselves. Of course if you notice them fighting, you will need to separate the pair and try to re-pair them with another bird as soon as possible. While the majority of birds will accept the mate that you have selected and paired them with, not all will, and you may have to re-pair some of your birds several times before a compatible mate is found. Cockatiels are territorial, although not as much so as parakeets, but if you do find it necessary to separate and re-pair them, always move the female, as I believe her to be the more territorial of the sexes. If cage space permits, its best to move them both to another cage and re-pair each of them with another mate.

When putting young cockatiels to work, if they are not showing signs of nesting within 6 weeks, its probably best to go ahead and try to re-pair them with another mate. Cockatiels have a long breeding life, and once bonded, it's best to never separate them. Therefore, try to mate them in the beginning so they will produce the colors or traits that you desire for their entire life.

Working Your Nestboxes In Cage Breeding

Working your nestboxes with cage breeding is the same as it was with colony breeding. I guess the one exception will be that you probably will not need to mark the babies, as it will be easier to distinguish them from the adult birds simply because there are not as many birds in a cage as there are in a colony.

You can attach an index card to the outside of each nestbox and keep a detailed record of the production of each individual pair of birds. This allows you to see exactly which birds are your top producers, and it is the offspring from these select breeders that you will want to use for your future breeders.

Resting Your Birds In Cage Breeding

While many people who cage breed parakeets don't rest them, cockatiels have a much longer life span and I believe they need the rest. After your birds have produced 4 or 5 clutches in a row, you will probably notice the clutches beginning to get smaller as well as you may also begin to notice a decline in the quality of the chicks, and it is at that time that you will want to consider resting them for a couple of months. Timing is an important factor to consider when resting your birds. The demand and prices are usually down in the hot summer months, and that is the logical time to give them a rest. Breaking your birds up is the same in cage breeding as in colony breeding. Start removing all fresh laid eggs and when the last chick emerges you will have an empty nestbox. Either remove the nest or seal the hole. The hen will then stop laying and the pair will take their much needed rest, enabling them to replenish their system for the next breeding season.

The greatest backyard business ever!

Chapter 11

Breeding Lovebirds

Breeding Lovebirds In Colonies

There are a number of different types of lovebirds that are profitable to breed for the pet market, but the most popular ones continue to be the peachface, bluemask, blackmask and fisher lovebirds. Of these four, the peachface is the easier to breed and would be the logical choice for the beginner to start with. Lovebirds are an extremely tough little bird for their size and can be successfully bred in either cages or colonies, but there appears to be a larger percentage of commercial breeders that choose the colony method.

Allowing 1.5 square feet of floor space per bird, an 8'x 10' breeding pen would hold around 25 pair per pen. A smaller pen will work fine, but a pen larger than 80 square feet is not recommended, nor is it recommended to have over 1.5 birds per square foot of floor space. Experience has shown that overcrowding will just cause a lot

A colony of black masked lovebirds.

of quarreling, resulting in less production, not more. Lovebirds have very strong beaks and love to chew, so make sure you construct your pens with ½" x 1" welded wire or ½" x ½" hardware cloth. Each pen will need to have plenty of perch space. Perches can be made from 1"x 2" or 2"x 2" planks, or ½" dowel rods.

A couple of peachface lovebird colonies.

Lovebird Nestboxes

Whether you buy or build your own nestboxes, make sure they are made out of at least 3/8" thick plywood, as anything less will be reduced to rubble in short order. Dimensions can vary, but an ideal size is 8"x 8"x 8" or 8"x 8"x 10"tall with a 2" hole in the front. In fact, it's a good idea to have both sizes in your pen to give the birds a choice of nesting boxes. It's not necessary for the nestboxes to have perches on them as the birds can fly in and out with ease, but if you purchase nestboxes that already have perches attached, you need not remove them. Most likely, the birds will chew them off in time anyway. To avoid removing your nestboxes for weekly inspections, hang them at eye level or slightly lower and this will allow you to look inside without having to take them down.

Unlike parakeets or cockatiels, lovebirds require a nesting material, and will build somewhat of a nest inside of the nestbox. Lovebird eggs seem to require a higher level of humidity than the eggs of many other birds, and it is for that reason that its good to provide nesting material that contains a little moisture. If you happen to live in an area where you can get a supply of fresh palm fronds, those are excellent, or the fresh small branches from willow, apple, cherry or other nonpoisonous trees are also readily accepted. The birds will strip the bark from the branches and use it to build their nest inside the box. Alfalfa hay also makes a suitable nesting material, as will other grasses and leaves. You can place a little nesting material in the nestboxes to start things off, but the bulk of the nesting material needs to be placed inside the pen and let the birds choose their own nestboxes and build their own nest. The birds seem to like it better if the nesting material is not just thrown in the pen, but put in something that will hold it up off the floor, such as a wire basket fashioned out of the ½"x 1" welded wire used in the construction of the breeding pen.

Feeding And Watering Lovebirds

Each breeding colony of birds will need a feeding station as well as some type of watering system. If you have very many colonies of birds, it will be a big timesaver if you have one of the low-pressure automatic water systems that are on the market today. If not, the poultry drinking base that screws on to a jar and is inverted works fine.

Homemade feed stations such as these work fine for lovebirds.

Use separate feed pans for the basic seed mix and supplemental feed.

Your feeders can be the self-feeding type manufactured for poultry that will hold a weeks supply of feed, or they can be something as simple as an open tray or pan. The lovebird diet consist mainly of several different types of seed which are supplemented with a vitamin/mineral mix as well as fresh fruit or vegetables. Lovebirds will do well if fed a parakeet mix consisting of 50% white proso millet, 40% canary seed and 10% oat groats. In addition to the parakeet mix, sunflower seed can be fed in a separate feeder, or, as an option, many feed companies offer a cockatiel/lovebird mix, which is a blend of the above seeds. Those blends will work fine, provided the seeds are mixed in the proper ratio and the blend is not loaded up with cheaper quality millets.

There are a number of vitamin/mineral supplements on the market today that are commercially manufactured for pet birds, and because of the higher nutritional requirements that breeding birds require, it is strongly recommended that you use one of those products. In addition, many breeders will offer game bird starter or turkey starter to their breeding birds in a separate dish. Both game bird and turkey starter are higher in protein than the seed diet, as well as they include the necessary vitamins and minerals that a strictly seed diet is lacking in. Unfortunately, lovebirds do not readily take to these pelleted feeds, so a seed diet remains the main staple of their diet.

While raising babies, the addition of fresh fruit or vegetables to the diet is helpful and beneficial. Shredded carrots or fresh corn work great, although fresh corn can sometimes be expensive when not in season. Corn, either cracked or whole kernel, such as is fed to other types of livestock, can be boiled until soft and fed as a substitute, and is very inexpensive. Carrots can be bought wholesale in 50 pound bags and are usually not very expensive. Feed only the amount of soft foods such as these that the birds will consume within an hour or so, and it's a good idea that you feed it at the same time each day, as they will soon learn to wait for it to feed to the babies. Soft food works great to mix with a vitamin/mineral supplement, and by doing so, you will be assured your birds are getting the vitamins and minerals that breeding birds need.

Lovebirds have no teeth with which to chew their food and the addition of grit enables the gizzard to more efficiently grind the food to a consistency that makes the digestion and absorption of their diet more complete. There are several types of grit available, including ground granite and ground oyster shell. Ground oyster shell of baby chick size works great, and it also provides a good source of calcium. Since lovebirds husk their seed and eat only the inside of the kernel, be sure you have feed in the feeders and not a feeder full of husk.

Lovebirds also need a mineral block in each breeding pen to help supply the necessary calcium and phosphorus needed to make their eggshells. Breeding females require considerable more calcium than do non- breeding birds, and a diet that is lacking the proper amount will result in the laying hens pulling the needed calcium from their bones. This can result in soft shelled eggs and birds that develop rickets, in both chicks and adults. The mineral blocks will also help the birds to keep their beaks trimmed.

Feeding is most heavy during the first hour of the day as well as the last hour of their day, but it is very important that you keep feed before your lovebirds at all times. Birds are nibblers by nature, and will feed many times during the course of a day, especially when they have young in the nest.

Breeding Age Of Lovebirds

Lovebirds will begin breeding at somewhere around 6 to 8 months of age if they have been provided with a proper diet as well as an environment suitable to breeding, although many breeders prefer to hold them till they are 9 to 10 months before allowing them to breed.

Sexing Your Lovebirds

Although some species of lovebirds can be visually sexed with a high degree of accuracy, peachface, bluemask, blackmask and fisher lovebirds do not fall into that category. The fact that they are so difficult to sex poses one of the largest obstacles to breeding them successfully. Lovebirds can be DNA or surgically sexed with 100% accuracy, but the cost of having the procedure done can sometimes exceed the value of the bird itself. A combination of the following characteristics is helpful in determining the sex of lovebirds, although no single one is ever foolproof. In short, lovebirds are just plain hard to sex accurately.

- Males tend to be slightly more colorful than females, especially around the head.
- Females tend to be slightly larger than males.
- Females tend to bite harder than males.

- Most of the time it will be the female that carries the nesting material to the nestbox, although this is not always 100% correct.
- Females will often have a stockier, heavier build than the males and will have a wider stance when sitting on a perch than does the male.
- The pelvic bones of the female will be slightly wider apart and more flexible on the female than on the male. Once the female has laid an egg, this is one of the more reliable ways in which to accurately determine the true sex of the bird.

In summary, short of DNA or surgical sexing, any other means of sexing these varieties lovebirds is less than 100% accurate. Sexing lovebirds remains one of the more difficult aspects of breeding them successfully. **See Color Plate #3...page133**

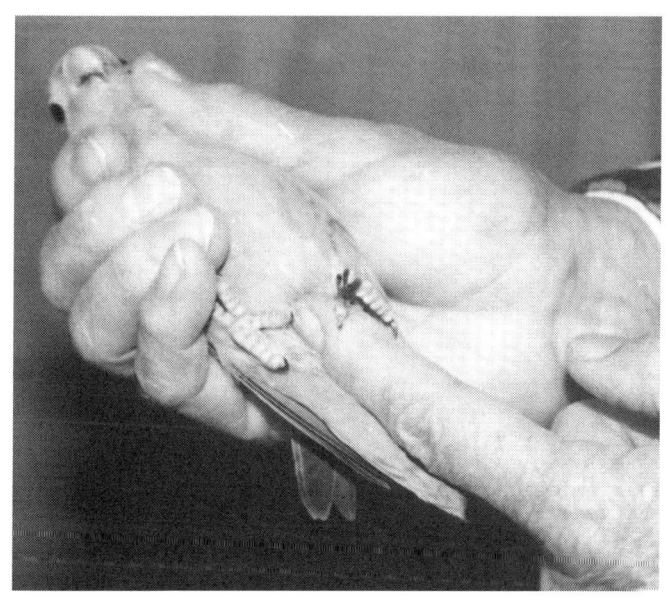

Lovebirds are very hard to accurately sex. To pelvic sex a lovebird, hold the bird in one hand and place the index finger on the bird's breastbone. Gently slide the finger down the breastbone towards the vent. You will feel two tiny bones in the area of the vent. If the bones almost touch, chances are it's a male. The pelvic bones of the female will be slightly wider apart than those of a male. This method is much more accurate after the bird has laid an egg.

The greatest backyard business ever!

Determining The Age Of Lovebirds

Adult lovebirds are very difficult to age. After the bird reaches a year or so of age, it's next to impossible to tell if it is one year old or five, and it is for that reason why it is so important to start with baby birds. That is the only way that you can know for certain the true age of lovebirds. Young juvenile birds will be of a paler color than the adult birds. Juveniles will usually be slightly smaller, although the young offspring from large breeding stock can sometimes be as large as adult birds of a smaller stock. Younger birds will usually have blackish streaks in the beak that will disappear as the bird matures. Older birds will have more rugged, worn looking nails, feet, legs and beaks.

Putting Your Lovebirds To Work

Once your birds become of age and you feel you have sexed them properly, it will be time to put them to work. Determine the amount of pairs that your breeding pens will hold using the formula of 1.5 square feet of floor space per bird, remembering not to allow more than around 25 pair to a pen. Lovebirds are territorial and will do a degree of quarreling when pairing up, therefore, the smaller size colonies will give you better control over your birds.

Allowing 30% to 50% more nestboxes in a pen than is required will give your birds a better selection of suitable nesting sites and will speed up the breeding process. Always hang all of the nestboxes at the same time that you plan on putting in a pen, never adding additional boxes or birds during the breeding season.

It has been my experience that lovebirds do not go to nesting quite as quickly as do parakeets and cockatiels, so don't get discouraged if the birds don't immediately go to work. Once the nest is built and the laying starts, the female will lay an egg every other day until she lays her entire clutch. She will normally start incubating the eggs after the second egg is laid, and they will hatch in the same order in which they were laid, every other day. Normal clutch size is from 4 to 6 eggs. Because some hens sit tighter and longer on their eggs than others do, incubation times will vary from between 22 to 24 days. Although the male spends time in the nestbox, it is the female who does the sitting on the eggs.

Once the chicks start to hatch, the female hardly leaves the nest. The male feeds her, and she, in turn feeds the newly hatched chicks. She produces a colostrum like substance known as crop milk, which she feeds to the youngest chicks. As the chicks grow, she increases the amount of partially digested feed that she gives them, reserving the crop milk for only the youngest of the chicks. Eventually the chicks are old enough that the male will bypass feeding her and directly feed the baby chicks himself.

Baby lovebirds grow extremely fast and will begin to leave the nestbox by the time they are five to six weeks of age. Because of their rapid growth, they must never be without feed. Once they leave

Baby lovebirds grow incredibly fast.

the nestbox, it is best to leave them in the breeding pen with the adult birds for another week or so, since the male will continue to feed them until they are fully weaned.

Working Your Nestboxes

Once you have put your birds to work, you will need to schedule yourself enough time to go through your breeding pens and check each nestbox a couple of times a week. Lovebirds are much more hyper and high strung than are cockatiels and parakeets, although they will still allow the inspection of their nestboxes, but extra care should be taken when working lovebirds. Gently raise the lid and take a look inside the box to see if it is being used, and if so, what stage the nesting process is in.

With young lovebirds, the first clutch of eggs will sometimes be infertile and these eggs will need to be removed so the pair will start another clutch quicker than they normally would. Incubation time for lovebirds will vary a little, depending upon how tight the hen sits on the eggs, but will usually be around 22 to 24 days. If the eggs don't appear fertile after 14 to 16 days of incubation, they should be removed. During incubation, a fertile egg will become slightly darker than a fresh egg and will have an ever so slight bluish color to it, due to the developing embryo inside the shell. Infertile or clear eggs as they are often called, will turn a slightly yellowish color and eventually become lighter in weight as the egg loses moisture and dries out. When the hen leaves the nestbox to go feed or get a drink, fertile eggs will retain heat much longer than will infertile eggs, provided they have been incubating for around 16 to 18 days, as the embryo itself is generating a degree of heat at that stage. In time, you will easily be able to distinguish fertile from infertile eggs.

Occasionally you will have lovebirds that are messy feeders and will plaster the crop milk all over the face of the tiny chicks. This substance will harden like glue if left for a long period, and subsequent feedings will result in an ever increasing buildup on the face of the chick, which if not removed, will result in a deformed beak rendering the bird somewhat worthless. It is easily removed if caught early, and is one of the reasons that frequent checking of the nestboxes is essential.

Another problem sometimes encountered when working nestboxes is a "wet nestbox". The normal droppings of lovebirds are not overly loose and will usually dry rather quickly. However, once in a while a pair of birds will have chicks that produce abnormal amounts of large, loose stools, resulting in a buildup within the nestbox of wet droppings. These abnormal droppings can be caused by anything as simple as too much soft food in the diet, or too much of an intake of water(which can happen if your building gets too hot), to something much more severe such as a bacterial infection. Many times the chicks in a wet nestbox will have the droppings accumulate and harden on their feet. These hardened droppings can get as hard as concrete and will result in deformed feet or toes and should be removed before the buildup gets to that point.

There will be times when you will lose a baby chick in the nestbox, and removing it before it starts to decompose is just another reason why its important to go through your nestboxes often. If the clutch is a large one, containing in excess of 6 babies, the last chick to hatch can be a good candidate to get trampled by the older nestlings. Most lovebirds will make good foster parents, and if possible, it is a good idea to transfer some of the smaller chicks from the larger clutches to smaller clutches that contain chicks of about the same age. Always transfer the younger ones when fostering chicks, preferably chicks less than 2 weeks of age. Older chicks that are fostered out will have a tendency to jump out of the nestbox, which will often result in their loss. Fostering excessively large clutches helps to even up the workload among your breeders, and can usually increase your annual production somewhat. Fostering eggs can also be done, as long as you transfer the eggs to another nest that has eggs in approximately the same stage of incubation. For instance, you would not want to transfer an egg that is ready to hatch to a nest that contains freshly laid eggs.

By the time the last chick leaves the nestbox, it's not uncommon for the hen to have already started laying another clutch of eggs. Sometimes the birds will re-line their nest with fresh nesting material, sometimes not. Its important to keep some fresh nesting material available throughout the breeding season, allowing the birds to rebuild their nest between clutches if they so choose. Lovebirds will occasionally change nesting sites between clutches, and it is for that reason that it is recommended to have plenty of extra nestboxes available in each breeding colony.

Every couple of weeks you will need to catch the young birds that are old enough to be removed from the breeding colony and transfer them into holding pens or cages until they are ready to go to market. By banding the adult birds before the breeding season begins, it is much easier to distinguish the adults from the youngsters. Banding with numbered bands is also an excellent way to keep track of the age of your lovebirds.

With colony breeding, it is difficult to keep accurate records of the production of individual breeding pairs, but you should at least keep a record of the production of each individual pen.

Resting Your Lovebirds

Good quality lovebirds that are properly cared for are usually prolific and will breed 12 months out of the year, but their production numbers will go to falling off after they have produced around 4 clutches without a rest period, and you will also probably see a noticeable reduction in the quality of the baby birds being produced. These are signs that indicate your birds are ready for a rest. Your production should be timed so as to give your birds a rest during the hot summer months, as demand and price are usually at the lowest levels of the year during the months of June, July and August. The demand for pet birds usually falls off right after Mothers Day, and doesn't resume its full strength until after school starts back in the fall. Good management would suggest that you not rest all of your birds at one time, lest you have no income during those months. You might rest 75% of your birds during the slow season, and after those birds get back into full production in the fall, break the remaining pairs up and give them a couple of months rest.

Once the decision is made to rest the birds, it's not an instant thing, but a gradual process that will take a couple of weeks to complete. As you work your nestboxes, simply start removing any freshly laid eggs and in a few weeks all of the remaining nestlings will have left the nest and your boxes will be empty. At that time, you can either remove the nestboxes from the pen or turn them around backwards so the birds cannot enter through the hole. With the absence of a suitable nesting site, your birds will then stop laying and take their much needed rest. Boxes should then be cleaned of the old nesting material and made ready for the next breeding cycle. A six or eight week rest is all that is needed if you are furnishing an adequate diet. After the rest period, you just start the whole breeding process over again.

By giving the birds a rest, you will extend their breeding life considerably as well as producing a much better quality chick. Lovebirds can live for 10 to 15 years, and can no doubt produce for most of that time, but clutches will become smaller and quality will decline as they grow older. For maximum production, your birds should not be bred for more than 5 or 6 years before replacing them.

Cage Breeding Lovebirds

Peachface, blackmask, bluemask and fisher lovebirds can all be successfully bred in cages. Peachface lovebirds come in a variety of colors, including the normal peachface, blue peachface, lutino peachface and light and heavy pied peachface. One important advantage of cage breeding lovebirds is the control that one has in producing these various colors. Of course supply and demand dictates the price, but some years there will actually be as much as 50% to 100% difference in the prices these different colors will fetch.

Although the most popular way to breed lovebirds in cages is with one pair per cage, it is possible to have several pair in a larger cage.

The Cage Breeding Unit

Lovebird cages can be purchased or homebuilt. Homebuilt cages should be constructed with ½" by 1" welded wire, making sure to grind smooth all sharp burrs from the openings have been cut for the doors and feeders. Single pair cages should be no smaller than 18" deep by 18" tall by 30" long. A larger cage of 36" deep by 36" tall by 48" long will house about 3 pair. Each cage will need some type of tray or catch pan underneath that will catch the seed husk and other litter. Many feed stores or aviary supply companies sell cages that are these sizes and they will work for all of the species listed in this book. These manufactured cages are stackable and usually include a metal tray for catching the droppings and seed husk. Cages will need ½" dowel rods at both ends to be used for perches. If you plan to have a lot of cages, consider an automatic watering system. It is money well spent. Nestboxes are the same with cage breeding as with colonies.

A successful lovebird breeding operation using cages.

Feeding

The feeding program with cages is the same as with colonies, with one exception. Birds bred in cages do not get the same amount of exercise as birds that are bred in colonies get, and they will have a tendency to become overly fat if given free choice sunflower or safflower seed. Overly fat birds will not reproduce well and your production and profits will suffer as a result. That being the case, it is best to feed the mix that has the sunflower or safflower seed already included in it rather than giving the birds an unlimited, free choice supply of those high fat content seeds. Of course you will need to keep available the same vitamin-mineral supplements, mineral blocks, and grit that was discussed in colony breeding.

Breeding Age Of Lovebirds In Cages

Lovebirds will often start to laying at an earlier age in cages than they will in colonies. I suppose that is because there is less distractions in cages than in colonies, as colonies are usually more crowded. Between 6 to 9 months old is a good age at which to put lovebirds to work in cages.

Putting Your Birds To Work In Cages

The tricky part of putting lovebirds to work in cages is making sure you have a pair, whereas in colonies, there is some room for error. Once the birds reach breeding age, simply pair them according to the colors that you are hoping to produce, and hang the nestbox. Provide the same nesting material as in colony breeding. Lovebirds will sometimes fight aggressively if they are not compatible, and you may have to re-pair your birds a time or so before they accept the mate you have chosen. Once a pair has bonded, its best to leave them together for the rest of their breeding life.

Working Your Nestboxes In Cages

Working the nestboxes with cage breeding is no different than with colony breeding. Since your nestboxes will hang outside the cage, you can attach index cards to them and keep accurate production records of each individual breeding pair. As the nestlings begin to emerge from the nest, make sure they are eating on their own before you remove them from the breeding cage.

Resting Your Lovebirds In Cages

As in colony breeding, timing is important. Rest your birds in the summer months, when prices and demand are usually the lowest. Breaking them up in cage breeding is the same as with colony breeding. By removing all of the freshly laid eggs, when the last chick leaves the nestbox, it will be empty. Either seal the hole or remove the box completely and the female will stop laying and both birds will take their much needed rest. As in colony breeding, if you have a sizeable amount of birds, it is best not to rest them all at one time, but rest them in stages. By resting your birds on a rotating basis, you will have a steadier flow of income throughout the year.

Chapter 12

Breeding Zebra Finches

Breeding Zebra Finches In Colonies

The Zebra finches are among the most popular and affordable of all finch species. They are very social little birds, rarely exhibiting aggressive behavior, and it is my belief that they do best in a colony breeding situation. Zebra finches are perhaps the bird of choice for beginners to start with, because they are such a hardy little bird and they are so prolific. In fact, their urge to reproduce is so great that oftentimes they will build another nest right on top of an existing clutch of eggs, even before the first clutch hatches.

An 8' x 10' pen is an ideal size and will accommodate around 65 pair of zebra finches. Although a smaller pen will work fine, a pen larger than 80 square feet is not recommended, nor is a pen that is much longer than 10' in length. The longer the pen is the harder it will be for you to catch the birds when it comes time to market them. When figuring the amount of birds that a pen will hold, use .6 square feet (6/10) of floor space per bird as a formula. Since zebra finches are not really an aggressive bird, people will sometimes have a tendency to overcrowd them. Overcrowding finches will cause feather picking and stress, and will decrease, not increase your production.

Finches do not gnaw or chew as the hookbills do, and this allows the breeding pens to be constructed with a less durable material. Screen wire or hardware cloth will suffice, as will paneling on any solid walls you may have, but the pens will never be useful for breeding anything but finches if constructed with these types of lightweight materials. My recommendation would be to construct all pens with ½" x 1" welded wire or ½" x ½" hardware cloth and use 3/8" inch or heavier plywood for any interior walls, and this will allow the pens to be used for other species in the future if you should so desire. Provide plenty of perch space in each pen. Perches can be made from ½" dowel rods, 1"x 2" or 2"x 2" planks, or even tree branches.

Zebra Finch Nestboxes

When it comes to picking a suitable nesting site, zebra finches are perhaps the least picky of all birds and will nest just about anywhere in practically any type of nesting container or box. If you decide to build your own, a 5" x 5" plywood box is of sufficient size. A 1 ½" hole cut in the front works well, or some nextboxes will have the entire top 1/3 of the front side left open for an entrance.

Many feed stores or pet supply companies sell ready-made nestboxes or nesting cups that are made of plastic or wicker. Coffee cans, cardboard deli containers or butter dishes will all work well. The bottom line is that just about anything that you can hang on the wall, the birds will use for a nest.

In the wild, finches will build a nest in trees and shrubs instead nesting in hollow trees as parakeets and cockatiels do. Therefore, it is important that your birds have some type of nest building material available to them, even though you are still going to provide a nestbox. Zebra finches will build a nest out of just about anything that they can carry, but dried grass is the most commonly used material. Dried lawn clippings work well, especially Bermuda grass, or if you have a large amount of birds, the straw from a bale of hay will work. When using hay for nesting material, make sure that it is relatively fine hay and not too coarse, since they are such small birds and cannot carry large, coarse pieces of nesting material. While throwing the nesting material in the floor of the pen will work, many breeders prefer to fashion a wire basket to hold the nesting material up off the floor. I have had good results either way, but keeping the nesting material in a basket off the floor makes cleaning a little easier.

Feeding And Watering Zebra Finches

Each pen of birds will need its own feeding station and some type of watering system. There are a variety of automatic watering systems on the market today and they are definitely time savers. If you decide to go with one of the automatic systems, make sure that you select one that is suitable for birds as small as zebra finches. Some of the watering systems on the market require more pressure to operate than a tiny zebra finch is capable of exerting. The poultry drinkers that screw onto a jar and are then inverted work well for zebra finches, although they are somewhat messy, since the birds like to bathe in them. If you use the jar type drinkers, make sure that they are washed on a daily basis, otherwise a bacterial growth can buildup inside the jar which can cause some major problems with your birds. A lot of people have a tendency to overlook the importance of a clean, fresh water supply. Zebra finches consume a lot of water for birds their size, so make sure that their drinkers never run dry.

For feeders, you can use something as simple as a cake pan, or you can purchase a poultry type feeder that will hold a week or more supply of feed. Zebra finches are primarily seedeaters, although they will eat a few insects and mealworms. Much research has been done on the diets of poultry and gamebirds, but very little actual scientific research has been done on the diet of finches, therefore, most commercial finch raisers still continue to feed a basic seed mixture, supplementing it with various things in an attempt to provide somewhat of a balanced diet. Zebra finches husk their seed, eating only the inside of the kernel, so be careful that you have feed available in your feeders, and not a feeder full of seed husk. Finches are a very active little bird and have an extremely high metabolism, which makes it very important that they never be without feed, especially when raising their young.

The basic seed mix will consist of German millet, red and white proso millet, canary seed, oat groats and red Siberian millet. Although these seeds can be purchased separately, most raisers prefer not to mix their own, choosing instead to use one of the blends available from the major seed companies. If you choose a blend, make sure it has a large portion of the tiny German millet, since it is the grain that the birds prefer the most, while some of the cheaper quality mixes will contain a larger portion of the less expensive red or white proso millets.

In addition to the seed blend, you will need to keep before your birds at all times one of the commercial feed supplements such as "Birds Choice", "Petamine", "Nutricare", etc. These will help ensure that your finches get the essential vitamins, minerals and other trace elements that are lacking in a straight seed diet.

Green foods, such as clover, fresh alfalfa, spinach, rape, etc. all offer an excellent sources of vitamins and minerals, and can be fed when ever they are available.

Boiled eggs are a good source of calcium as well as animal protein for zebra finches and they will readily accept them, especially when they have young in the nest. The birds will eat shell and all, so there is no need to remove the shell, just break it up a bit, as it is one of the better sources for calcium. When feeding soft foods such as boiled eggs, its best to feed it on a consistent basis and to feed it at approximately the same time each day.

Boiled eggs will spoil rather quickly, especially in warm weather, so if you decide to feed them, its best to only put out what will be consumed within a couple of hours of time.

Zebra finches have no teeth with which to chew their food, so grit must be supplied to enable the gizzard to grind the seed to a consistency in which digestion can readily take place. Commercial grit made from either ground up oyster shell or ground up granite is available in different sizes. Zebra finches need to be supplied with the smallest size available, which is sometimes called baby chick grit.

We recommended mineral blocks in each breeding pen of parakeets, cockatiels, and lovebirds as a source of calcium, but zebra finches do not have the strong, sharp, hookbills that those birds have, and therefore are not capable of eating those hard type of mineral blocks. That is why it is so important to make sure they get their calcium requirements from sources such as fresh greens, ground oyster shell, egg shells, etc. Some feed stores carry calcium carbonate or bone meal, or other commercial calcium supplements that will also work. Cuttle fish bone is also an excellent source, but it is cost prohibitive to use on a commercial scale.

Zebra finches are nibblers by nature and will feed dozens of times throughout the day. They have an extremely high metabolism, with a heart rate of from 800-1200 beats per minute, and a respiratory rate of 140-200 per minute. Those numbers should convince anyone that these little birds should have feed available to them at all times, and it becomes even more important when young chicks are in the nest. Never, ever let your feeders run dry.

Breeding Age Of Zebra Finches

Zebra finches that are in good health are one of the most prolific species of birds that I know of. They will readily breed as early as 12 to 16 weeks of age, although it is a good idea to let them mature to around 5 to 6 months of age before allowing them to breed.

Sexing Zebra Finches

Zebra finches are quite easy to sex after they have gone through their first molt and shed their juvenile feathers. This will usually have occurred by the time they are 10 to 12 weeks old.

- **Normal gray males:** basic gray color, black band or bar on the chest, white spots on chestnut colored sides, orange cheek patches, and a bright red beak. Male zebra finches will sing, females will not.
- **Normal gray females:** lighter colored beak, with the rest of her body being a light gray color.

There are many Zebra finch color mutations, such as the white, that can only be sexed by the color of the beak, as they are absent of the breast barring, cheek patches and chestnut colored sides. Males will always have the brighter colored red beaks and will generally exhibit a brighter, more vivid overall color than the females. **See Color Plate#4...page133**

Determining The Age Of Zebra Finches

Once zebra finches go through their first molt and shed their juvenile feathers, it becomes increasingly difficult to tell exactly how old they are. They will usually go through this first molt at anywhere from 5 to 10 weeks of age. Prior to that, their plumage will usually resemble that of the adult female. Newly hatched chicks have a grayish colored beak that soon turns black. Because of this, young zebras are often referred to as "black bills". Instead of black bills, some of the chicks of the various colored mutations will have a pinkish colored beak upon hatching. As the chicks mature, the black or pink on the beak gradually gives way to the red coloration of the adults, with the male beak being the brighter colored red. By the time the chicks are 10 to 12 weeks old, there is usually none of the black left on the beak and at that time they are very difficult to distinguish from their parents.

Other secondary characteristics that adult birds have are larger and more worn looking feet, longer toenails, longer and rougher looking beaks, and overall larger body size. These secondary characteristics are not very reliable and it is next to impossible to know if a bird is one year old or four years old, and it is for that reason that a person is wise to only start out in this business with baby birds. That is the only absolute sure way of knowing their true age.

Putting Your Zebra Finches To Work

Once your birds reach breeding age, no doubt you will be eager to allow them to begin the process of hatching and raising their young. Determine the amount of pairs your pen will hold using the formula of .6 square feet (6/10) of floor space per bird. Zebra finches are very social little birds and are not overly quarrelsome when pairing up, but it is still a good idea to have a few extra males in each pen to give the females a better selection as they begin choosing their mates. Extra males are all right, just don't allow extra females in a pen. If after you pair all your birds up, you still have females left over, sell them. Putting extra females in a pen will usually create problems, due to the fact that they are the more aggressive of the two genders.

Since zebra finch nestlings grow and mature so fast, it's a good idea to put legbands on the adult birds as a way of insuring that you can tell the adults from the juveniles. Band the males on one leg and the females on the opposite leg. Since you will inevitably loose some adults through the course of the breeding cycle, the leg banding method will allow you to keep track of what was

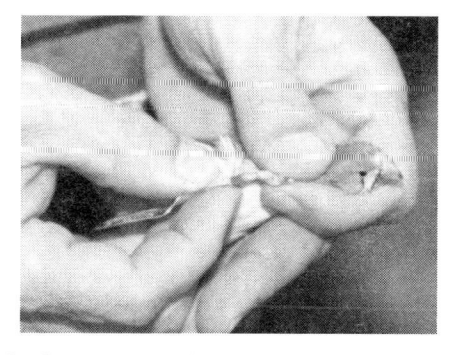

The greatest backyard business ever!

lost, male or female. Most of the time when you find a dead bird on the floor, it will have had the feathers picked to the point that identification is not possible.

Zebra finches are not at all choosy about a picking a nesting site, but it is still a good idea to hang approximately 20% more additional nesting containers in each pen than is required. Be sure and hang all of them in the breeding pen at the same time, since adding nesting containers at a later date can create problems, as will adding additional birds.

In my opinion, zebra finches are undoubtedly one of the easiest and most prolific of all birds to raise, and provided they have been on an adequate nutritional program and are of the proper age, they will almost immediately start building a nest when nesting materials are made available. Zebra finches will quickly build a nest on their own, but you can normally speed the process up even more by placing a hand full of nesting material in each nesting container, be it a nestbox, coffee can, butter dish, or whatever. They will then continue carrying nesting material to the nest, with the male doing most of the carrying and the female helping out with the actual construction and fashioning of the nest. The nest is usually built within a week to ten days, and soon afterwards the first eggs will appear.

Many zebras are so zealous and consumed with the prospects of rearing a family that its not at all uncommon for a couple of eggs to be laid and then the birds will start building another nest right on top of those freshly laid eggs, which, of course will lead to the loss of those first few eggs. There is not a lot that can be done to discourage this overly enthusiastic urge to reproduce, other than after the majority of your birds have started laying, you can cut back on the amount of nesting material available for new nest construction. There does, however, need to be a limited amount available at all times as they will often re-line their nest between clutches.

Zebra finches normally lay around 4 to 6 eggs, but it is not at all uncommon to have 7 or 8 eggs per clutch. If you start to noticing more eggs than that in a nest, it usually means that two females are using the same nest. There is nothing you can do if that happens, other than make sure you have ample nestboxes in the pen. The hen will usually lay an egg every day, but she will usually wait until after the third or fourth egg is laid before she starts incubating them. Both male and female will incubate the eggs, although the female does the most of it. The male will usually occupy the nest at night along with the female. Incubation time is from 12 to 16 days, with 14 days being the most common. Some hens will sit tighter on the eggs and leave the nest less often than others, and that explains why some clutches will hatch sooner than others.

Hatching of the eggs will not all occur at the same time, since the eggs that were the last to be laid do not have the same amount of incubation time as the first few that were laid, although there will not usually be a great deal of difference. The young are extremely tiny when they hatch and are blind, helpless and covered with fuzzy, downy feathers. Both parents share in the feeding responsibilities of the newly hatched chicks. The growth rate of the freshly hatched

A zebra finch holding pen, sometimes called the bullpen. It's a good idea to keep a few extra males in the holding pen with young zebras during the weaning process.

chicks is truly remarkable, and it is a very demanding job on the parent birds. The chicks seem to double in size within the first few days and it is extremely important that the parent birds have feed available at all times. Their growth rate is such that by the time the chicks are three weeks of age, they will begin to leave the nest.

Some of the chicks will return to the nest at night to sleep, and for a few days to a week or so after the chicks leave the nest, the male will continue to feed them. They are usually fully weaned by the time they are five to six weeks old. By the time the last chicks leave the nest, the hen will more than likely have started laying a new clutch of eggs.

Since young zebra finches grow and mature so fast, they will need to be removed from the breeding colony within a month after they leave the nest, otherwise, they will become difficult to distinguish from the adults, which is why it's a good idea to band your adult birds.

Working Your Nestboxes

Once you have put your finches to work, you will need to schedule yourself enough time to go through your breeding pens and inspect their nest a couple of times a week to see how things are doing. Zebra finches are shy little birds and do not tolerate having their nest inspected as easy as do the parakeets, cockatiels or lovebirds covered earlier in this book, but nevertheless, they do need some attention. Since they build a nest within whatever type of nesting receptacle that you have made available, it's often difficult to actually see inside the nest itself. Fortunately, zebra finches are usually very good parents and don't require much outside help.

When checking the nest, usually the less handling that you can do the better off you will be. If the nest contains chicks that are 15 to 18 days old and you disturb them very much, the young birds will often jump out of the nest, and their survival rate is poor at that age. You can put them back in the nest, and 9 times out of 10 they will jump right back out. Therefore, it is best to just try to peek inside the nest to see what is going on and not handle the nest itself, if at all possible. Actually, about the only thing you are looking for is to see if there are any dead birds in the nest that would need removing. After your birds have raised several clutches of babies, the nesting material will sometimes need changing, but this can only be done if you are able to replace it at just the right time; just as the last chicks leaves the nest and before the hen has started laying again.

In the case of parakeets, cockatiels and lovebirds, it was suggested that you could combine clutches or foster chicks from larger clutches to the smaller clutches as a way to increase production. Since zebra finches don't consent to inspection of their nest very well, it is not recommended to foster babies unless absolutely necessary. For the most part, it's best just to let nature take its course if you are breeding zebra finches on a commercial scale. You will find that zebra finches are one of the easiest of all birds to breed in captivity and need no outside help.

Resting Your Birds

After your birds have raised 4 to 6 clutches of babies, you will notice that the production as well as the quality of birds being produced will begin to falter. It's a good idea to give them a rest at that time and allow them to replenish and rebuild themselves.

Bird raisers use the term "breaking up" when referring to removing the nestboxes and forcing their birds to take a rest. The demand for pet birds is usually slower in the summer months than at any other time of the year, which will usually result in lower prices in the summer. It only makes sense to give your birds a rest during that time. Plan on resting your birds during the months of June and July, putting them back to work around mid August, so as to be back in full production by the end of September. Prices usually pick up in the fall after school starts back. It's not a good idea to have all your birds broke up at one time, so I recommend only breaking up around 75% of them in the summer, giving the others a rest at some other time of the year. That, of course means 75% of your pens, not 75% of the birds in a given pen. Always having some of your birds working will enable you to have a steadier income throughout the year.

To break your birds up, simply start checking the nest and when you find a nest without chicks, begin removing any freshly laid eggs. Over the course of a couple of weeks, all of the babies will have emerged from the nest and if you have been removing the freshly laid eggs, all of the nest will be empty. That's the time to remove the nest from the pens and the birds will stop laying and take their rest. Usually a 6 to 8 week rest will be sufficient time for them to recharge their batteries and be ready to go again.

Throughout the course of breeding season, you will have lost a certain amount of adult birds from various causes. It's natural and it's just going to happen. However, at the beginning of a new breeding season, you will need as close to equal amounts of males and females in each breeding pen as is possible. Before you put the nest back up after the rest period, you will need to catch all the birds in each pen and re-count the males and females, and add or subtract birds to the pen as needed before hanging the nesting containers back up after their rest period.

Zebra finches have a life span of 5 to 7 years, and will reproduce for most of that time. After they have produced for 3 years, their production will fall off noticeably. They will have fewer clutches per year with fewer chicks per clutch, and it is for that reason that it makes good economic sense to replace them after their third year with younger birds. I have found that the second year of production is usually the best.

Cage Breeding Zebra Finches

Zebra finches will breed well in individual cages, but for the commercial producer it is not really feasible to breed them individually, since they do so well in colonies. However, some do elect to cage breed zebra finches when experimenting with genetics and concentrating on developing specific color varieties. Cages can be purchased, or if homemade, should be constructed with ½" x 1" welded wire. ½" dowel rods make the best perches. A cage 12" x 12" by 15" long make an ideal size finch breeding cage. An automatic water system is great if you plan a very large setup. The diet, maturity rate, nesting behavior and recommended breeding cycles of zebra finches are the same with the cage breeding method as they are with the colony breeding method.

An extremely nice combination setup of cage and colony breeding zebra finches.

The greatest backyard business ever!

Chapter 13

Health Problems

Maintaining good health in your birds will depend to a large degree on the type of hygiene, diet, and environmental factors that you provide, as well as heredity. Hygiene, diet and environmental factors can be largely controlled by the commercial bird breeder, whereby heredity is a much more complicated issue. We most often think of inherited qualities as the simple things such as size and color, but it actually covers a much broader scope, not the least of which is the resistance to certain types of diseases. That, in turn, will lead to the study of genetics, of which a lot is yet to be learned when we are referring to exotic bird genetics.

Recognizing a disease or problem when it first occurs is of utmost importance to the commercial bird raiser who is depending on deriving part or all of his or her lively hood from the profits of this business. Because commercial bird breeders often have hundreds or thousands of birds in close confinement, if disease strikes, it can sometimes spread throughout the entire flock in a relatively short time. Make every effort to handle any health problems before they are allowed to get out of hand.

Characteristics Of A Sick Bird

- Lethargic, listless, droopy looking
- Depression
- Fluffed plumage
- Loss of appetite
- Loss of weight…going light
- Head tucked under wing
- Diarrhea
- Clicking, rattling respiratory sounds
- Rapid, labored breathing
- Swollen, puffy eyes
- Discharge from nasal passage

A bird that is obviously sick should be quickly isolated from the other birds and placed in a hospital cage. A good hospital cage should consist of a cage with a 250-watt infrared light that is suspended the proper distance above the cage so that the temperature on the perch will range between 85 and 95 degrees Fahrenheit. Make sure that the rays from the heat lamp only covers about half of the perch. This will allow the bird to get out of the heated area if it so desires. Feed and water should be on the floor of the cage at all times.

Sickly birds are usually reluctant to eat, and since birds have such a high metabolism, it is often starvation that leads to the death of the bird and not a disease in itself. Many times, the addition of the heat in a hospital cage will be all that is needed to bring a bird back to good health, provided of course that you are not dealing with a serious disease.

The majority of the diseases that affect parakeets, cockatiels, lovebirds and zebra finches, have such similar symptoms that it is difficult to diagnose them specifically without professional help. I do not feel qualified to give advice about diagnosing and treating the birds of others, but would rather encourage the commercial breeder to do everything possible in the area of nutrition, hygiene and environment to keep from having problems in the first place.

Small exotic birds can be difficult to treat for specific infectious diseases, even if the correct diagnosis is made. Many times when a bird begins to get sick, one of the first things to occur is a loss of appetite and thirst. That makes it rather difficult to medicate the birds through their feed or water. Whereby large birds such as parrots and macaws can be injected with medication, it is impractical to inject each bird in a flock of hundreds or thousands of small birds with medication several times a day.

When I first started breeding parakeets in 1975, there were very few veterinarians who specialized in, or even knew hardly anything at all about exotic birds. Fortunately, that is changing, although it can still be hard to find a veterinarian in any given area who knows a great deal about exotic birds. The desire just isn't there for most veterinarians to spend a lot of time specializing in birds, while the demand is so great for cats, dogs, horses, cattle, etc.

I do not propose to encourage the commercial bird breeder to become his/her own veterinarian. Not at all. On the contrary, I believe that once a problem is indicated, because you are a commercial breeder and derive income from your birds, that professional help should be sought without delay. If a qualified veterinarian is not available in your area to work with you, there is no need to despair.

During my 25 years in the exotic bird business, there were no veterinarians in my immediate area that really knew anything at all about exotic birds, and they were the first to admit it. I lived only a two hour drive from Texas A&M University, which has one of the leading colleges of veterinary medicine in the country. When I suspected a problem, I would drive or ship a specimen down to their veterinary medicine diagnostic laboratory. If a qualified veterinarian is not located in your area and you believe you are having a health problem with your birds, I suggest you contact a diagnostic lab at one of the colleges of veterinary medicine that will be willing to work with you. It is not necessary to live close to one, as you can usually ship a specimen by overnight express and the lab will have it the next day. My experiences with them have been positive. The appendix at the back of this book includes a state by state listing of Veterinary Diagnostic Laboratories.

Although it might sound somewhat harsh, many times the best thing to do with a sick bird is to humanely get rid of it. Sometimes that will prove to be the simplest and the most effective way to get rid of a small problem before it turns into a major headache. Commercial breeding of exotic birds is quite a bit different than breeding birds as a hobby or the keeping of a single bird as a pet. In commercial breeding, your entire livelihood can be at stake. Birds often respond poorly to treatment, and because commercial aviaries usually have hundreds or even thousands of birds confined in a single building, getting rid of the source of the problem can minimize the possibility of an epidemic running through the entire building. It's not at all uncommon in the poultry industry. Individual chickens, turkeys or game birds are rarely treated, they are destroyed, with the theory being that if you get rid of the bird, you have got rid of the problem. Actually, a lot of valuable information can be gleaned from the poultry and game bird industry, and much of it will be applicable to exotic birds as well. I suggest adding poultry and game bird books to your library of information.

Common Problems You May Encounter

Egg Binding

Occasionally a bird will be unable to expel a fully formed egg for different reasons. There are several things that can cause egg binding, such as an oversized, mis-shaped egg or a soft shelled egg. As a general rule, birds that are provided a balanced diet as well as an additional source of calcium, do not suffer from this problem, but, however, once in a while you will still find an egg bound hen. An unpassed egg in the cloaca prevents the bird from passing waste products, which will eventually result in toxemia and death. Usually you will find the afflicted female looking exhausted, fluffed up, sitting in the bottom of the cage or floor of the aviary, usually unable to fly. You may or may not see her straining to pass the egg. Upon catching the hen, you can simply turn her upside down and using the index finger, gently feel the abdominal area above the birds cloaca or vent. If she is egg bound, you will easily be able to feel the egg.

Heat will often be the only thing that is necessary to help the hen pass the egg. Although the hospital cage with the heat lamp will sometimes work, it is best if the hen is placed in a perchless cage or box with a heating pad placed on the floor. The cage or box will need to be of the proper size that the heating pad will cover the entire floor, forcing the bird to sit on the heated area. The heating pad should be adjusted to a warm, but not hot temperature. Putting a few drops of mineral oil into the cloaca with a tiny eyedropper can be done to help lubricate the passage of the egg. Sometimes just sitting on the heating pad for a couple of hours will do the trick and the hen will pass the egg. Heat works wonders with birds, just make sure the heat isn't too high.

In the event she does not pass the egg within a few hours, it may become necessary to manipulate the egg by using manual pressure to help her expel the egg. A few more drops of mineral oil inserted into the vent with a small eyedropper will be helpful. Holding the bird in one hand, gently apply pressure and massage or work the egg downward with the fingers of the other hand. This must be done in a very slow and deliberate manner and will usually result in the expulsion of the egg. At that point it is a good idea to return her to the hospital cage for a day or so before returning her to her cage or flight pen.

A second egg binding by the same female should mark the end of her breeding career for you.

Molting

Molting can be defined as the normal loss and replacement of feathers, and should not be confused with an illness. Most adult birds will molt on a gradual scale and it will not be that noticeable. The most noticeable changes will be seen in the youngsters, as they shed their first feathers and replace them with their more colorful adult feathers. It is not until after this first molt that many birds can accurately be sexed. Again, normal molting is not a problem. I only mention it here because I have had newcomers in the business to panic, mistaking the normal shedding of feathers for a possible disease.

Quite often, when birds are broken up and forced to end their breeding cycle they will go through a molt, especially if the daylight hours are shortened. New feather growth requires plenty of protein, so it is important to continue your resting birds on a quality ration.

French Molt

French molt is a feather abnormality that is mainly seen in parakeets, and it is quite different than the normal molt. It usually appears at about the time the young birds get ready to leave the nest. It is sporadic in occurrence and may or may not affect all of the birds in a particular clutch. It is easily recognized by excessive shedding of the wing and tail feathers. Often the affected birds will be unable to fly and are referred to as "crawlers", "runners", or "creepers" by bird buyers. If they are not extremely affected, and have lost only their tail and primary wing feathers, they actually can be quite cute, and will remind you of a tiny penguin. The actual cause of French molt is not known, and there is no known cure. Although you will occasionally have a bird to show up with this feather abnormality, French molt isn't a major concern with most breeders. I only mention it so that you will know what it is if you see it.

While the young affected birds will usually grow new feathers, this will take around six weeks or so, and by that time they are considered adult birds by the pet trade, and in the case of parakeets, they will not bring the premium price that young birds bring. Those birds that do grow new feathers should never be used for breeding purposes, although they can still make good pets.

Diarrhea

Diarrhea is normally associated with a disease, and is not a disease in itself. It should not be confused with the loose, watery stools that a stressed bird may have, such as when birds are being shipped. If nothing has been changed in the diet that could cause digestive upsets, diarrhea should be considered a clinical sign of a possible serious problem within the aviary. Removal of the bird should be immediate, as it could be the start of a contagious disease. If a number of birds are showing this symptom, professional help should be considered, as there are many possible causes. Microscopic examination of the droppings could reveal something such as internal parasites, which can spread rapidly in a colony breeding operation, or cultures may need to be grown from the various organs to determine the probable cause. Regardless of the cause, the presence of true diarrhea in birds should not be taken lightly, especially if you notice several birds exhibiting the same problem.

Overgrown or Deformed Beaks

Although it is not a common problem, occasionally this condition will develop. It's much more commonly in parakeets than in cockatiels, lovebirds or zebra finches, and if not corrected, it can sometimes become difficult, if not impossible for the bird to eat or feed its young. Toenail clippers can be used to trim the beak back to as near normal as possible. Its not hard to hold the bird up to the light and determine where the last bit of meat tissue or blood ends inside of the beak, since it will have a much darker color. Trim small pieces at a time to avoid getting into the blood supply. If you should accidentally cut into the blood supply and if the bleeding persists, it can usually be stopped with a styptic pencil.

Overgrown Nails

Overgrown nails will occasionally occur in zebra finches and parakeets, and much less frequently in lovebirds and cockatiels. It is quite easy to see where the blood supply ends in the nail, and it's a simple procedure using nail clippers to correct the problem. Be very careful not to cut into the blood supply, since the toe is on the lower extremity of the bird and quite a bit of bleeding can occur. In the event that you do accidentally cut into the blood supply, using a styptic pencil can help stop the bleeding. Left uncorrected, the nail can occasionally grow to the extent that it will cause deformity of the entire foot. That, in turn, can lead to fertility problems, as the female needs both feet firmly attached to the perch during the mating process.

External Parasites

External parasites include fleas, lice, mites, ticks, etc. By preventing wild birds and rodents entry into your aviary, external parasites will not normally be a problem. Birds will scratch and preen themselves regularly, but excessive scratching and restlessness with noticeable feather problems can be signs that you could possibly have mites or lice. Some are microscopic in size and will require examination of the bird or the feathers under a magnifying glass or microscope for a correct diagnosis. While external parasites can be a nuisance, disrupt breeding, and make some birds unsaleable, they rarely kill the bird. Poultry sprays are available to control external parasites, although they rarely create a problem if your premises are kept clean.

Internal Parasites

Internal parasites can be much more problematic than external parasites. Good hygiene and the elimination of wild birds and rodents are the best prevention. Many internal parasites have a lifecycle in which the eggs or the parasite itself is passed in the feces of the bird. These infected droppings then infect other birds. Keeping the floors dry and moisture free will help in breaking this cycle, as warmth and moisture are usually required for the eggs to survive. Birds that are cage bred will have less access to the feces of others, with the net result being that internal parasites are rarely seen in cage breeding operations.

Usually, when we think of internal parasites in birds, we think of the various types of worms, of which most are easily treatable with poultry wormers. However, there are protozoa type parasites such as giardia, coccidia, trichomonas, etc., which can really create some major problems within an aviary in short order. Fortunately, these are not at all common in parakeet, cockatiel, lovebird and zebra finch populations that are housed in clean aviaries. There are a number of anti-protozoal drugs that are effective in treating these types of internal parasites, but accurate identification of the bug is a must for correct treatment.

Although the outward looking symptoms of internal parasites can be identical to many bacterial infections, antibiotics used to treat bacterial infections are not effective against parasites and should not be used. Many times bird raisers will use a shotgun approach by using one of the broad spectrum antibiotics in an effort to treat problems that may arise in exotic birds. If you are lucky, this approach can work, but if not, more damage can be done as well as valuable time lost, possibly allowing the problem to get out of hand before a true diagnosis is made and treatment is started.

One of the best books that I have found that allows you to familiarize yourself with bird diseases is "Diseases of Birds", by L. Arnall and I.F. Keymer, published by T.F.H Publications, Inc., Neptune, N.J.

Although I believe that you should educate yourself and become familiar with bird diseases through reading and studying all available material, in most instances professional diagnosis should confirm a problem before treatment is administered. This is especially true for the beginner.

I suppose that just about any occupation has what is called "occupational hazards", and raising birds is no exception. There are certain diseases which humans can catch from birds and animals. Psittacosis is the most common disease that can affect both birds and humans, and humans can indeed catch the disease from infected birds. The clinical signs of the disease that are noticeable in birds can include labored and rattling sounds while breathing, diarrhea, lack of appetite, watery eyes, and nasal discharge, just to name a few. A psittacosis outbreak in a commercial bird aviary will lead to major production problems resulting in loss of income. Psittacosis is one of those types of diseases that can spread very rapidly in a flock of birds that are kept in confinement, and that is one of the main reasons that I sometimes suggest that for the commercial bird breeder, that often the best treatment for a sick bird is to quickly and humanely get rid of it. Economically, it can sometimes make the most sense.

Some very specialized laboratory test are required to confirm the presence of psittacosis in either birds or humans. The disease in birds can be treated with tetracycline, although treated birds can remain carriers. Humans can catch the disease from the infected bird by the breathing of dust in the air that contains the organism, or through the direct handling of the bird itself. In humans, it can produce a flu like symptom and is easily treatable with antibiotics. Since it is so rare in humans and the symptoms are so similar to the flu, if you ever go to the doctor with flu like symptoms, you would probably be wise to mention to the doctor the fact that you raise birds. Although it is very uncommon for humans to contract diseases from birds, I nevertheless, feel it important to make the reader aware that the possibility does exist.

Chapter 14
Managing And Upgrading Your Birds

While we have earlier listed and covered the basic management requirements such as housing, feeding, temperature, hygiene, lighting, rodent control, etc., a successful pet bird breeding operation will need to have the goal of continually replacing and upgrading the breeding stock.

Parakeets, cockatiels, lovebirds, and finches all have a different breeding life span in which they can be bred profitably. Although most of these birds will breed and raise offspring for their entire life, annual production falls off considerably as the birds grow older. Since expenses such as building upkeep, utilities, labor, etc. will all remain the same, it only makes good economic sense to keep the younger, more productive birds in your colonies or cages. A good management program will require that you hold back a certain amount of your offspring on a periodical basis for replacement breeders, and that you hold them back well in advance of the time that you will need them.

As an example, consider the profitable breeding life span of parakeets. Normally, colony bred parakeets that are rested once a year will give you three good years of production, with the second year usually being the best. A wise commercial parakeet producer will have a program of saving back enough offspring each year to replace at least one third of the flock. By doing that, the entire flock will be replaced every three years and you will continually have birds that are in their peak production years. Cage bred parakeets may have to be replaced even sooner. If parakeets are bred in cages and are not rested, they will usually not produce quite as long, as they will simply wear out quicker.

Saving back enough birds to replace the entire flock every three years may sound like a lot of your production, but on a percentage basis, it really isn't that much. Assuming that someone had a breeding operation consisting of 300 pair of breeders, holding back a third of them would mean 100 pair or 200 birds. Since you would invariably lose some birds during the growing and maturing process, and allowing a cushion for not having equal numbers of male and female birds, lets say you would need to hold back 225 birds from your production per year. If you refer back to Chapter 3 "Can I Make A Profit Breeding Birds" you will see that parakeets will average from 10 to 30 babies per pair per year. Using the middle average of 20 babies per pair, 300 pair of breeders would produce 6000 babies in a years time, and holding back 225 birds for replacement breeders would only be 3.75% of your annual production, or if you only averaged 10 babies per pair per year, you would still only need to hold back 7.5% of your annual production.

The time of the year as well as which year of production your birds are in should also be considered when holding back replacement breeders. In the case of parakeets, since the second season is usually the best, second year breeders would be the logical choice of birds in which to save babies from for replacement breeders. Additionally, offspring produced at the beginning or middle of the season will normally be stronger and hardier than the last clutches of the season.

One of the advantages of cage breeding parakeets or any other birds for that matter, is the fact that very accurate production records can be maintained on each individual pair of birds. Reproductive rates are but one of the qualities that offspring can inherit from past generations and it should be from your higher producers that you save future breed stock.

Although high production is one of the qualities that you should strive for, other things are also important. As an extreme example, it would make no sense to save offspring from breeders that had high production levels, but produced a degree of birds with feather problems such as French molt in each clutch.

Color is another factor that should be taken into consideration when holding back offspring for future breeders. I can remember a number of years back when there were so many green parakeets on the market that they became difficult to sell. Green is the dominant color of the parakeet, and that was the color that most people had for breed stock. Through the course of several years, people would hold back a higher percentage of their blues, pieds, albino and lutino parakeets for future breeders, since those were in short supply. Holding large amounts of those birds back for breeders created an even greater temporary shortage of those colors, with the result being that their prices soared. Wholesale prices on albino and lutino parakeets rose to as high as $10 each. Eventually, the supply of the rarer colored birds increased to the point that there was no longer a shortage of them and the prices came back down to within reason. Then some years later because so many breeders had converted over to the rarer colors, green birds actually became in short supply for awhile. I believe that it is best to breed for a variety of colors whether you are breeding parakeets, cockatiels, lovebirds or zebra finches, as that is what the market demands, although you will no doubt have your favorites.

The breeding of birds for specific colors, particularly parakeets and cockatiels, is extremely fascinating and interesting if done in a cage breeding operation where you have complete control over how the birds are paired up. Although I don't intend to cover the study of genetics in this book, it is, nevertheless, a fascinating study of inheritable characteristics. There are several good books that cover the subject of breeding for specific colors quite well. Encyclopedia of Budgerigars, by Georg A Radtke, Budgerigar Handbook, by Ernest H. Hart, and Encyclopedia of Cockatiel, by George A. Smith, all published by T.F.H. Publications, cover the breeding of parakeets and cockatiels for specific colors quite well.

While it should be the goal of every commercial bird producer to continually upgrade the flock, care should be exercised in acquiring breeding stock from outside sources. Of course, if a person has started out breeding birds on a very small scale and decides to expand, he will probably need to purchase additional breeding stock from others. However, each time additional birds are brought in, you run the risk of bringing a disease into your flock. That is why many large, established breeders of exotic birds maintain a closed aviary, meaning that they simply will not bring in additional breed stock for fear of introducing a disease into the flock and destroying their livelihood. Not only that, but many exotic bird breeders will not even allow visitors on their premises for fear of tracking in a disease. Again, we can learn many things from the poultry industry. They have taken these same type of measures for years and do not consider them extreme, but good management procedures.

Our Responsibility

While the breeding of pet birds can be fun and profitable, as the author of this book I feel that it is my responsibility to make anyone considering this business aware of the fact that there are moral obligations and responsibilities that go along with the breeding of pet birds, or any other animals for that matter.

I am a Christian and I believe in the theory of Creation. My Bible states in Genesis 1 that on the 5th day, God created the living creatures of this world. On the 6th day, He created man and gave him the authority to rule over "the fish of the sea and over the birds of the sky and over the cattle and over all the earth, and over every creeping thing that creeps on the earth."(Gen.1:26) I believe that along with the dominion and authority to rule that was given to us, comes a moral obligation to manage our birds and animals in a moral, humane and responsible manner.

Birds and animals were given to us to meet our needs as well as to enjoy. We eat cows and chickens, ride our horses, and keep cats, dogs, birds and fish in our homes to love and enjoy. Unfortunately, man has not always been the best manager of what he was given the authority to rule over. Many birds and animals are now extinct as a result of man's mismanagement. Because of urbanization and the loss of habitat worldwide, birds and animals are routinely put on the endangered species lists. Were it not for captive breeding, many others would soon join these lists. In all probability, the survival of many different species of both birds and animals will depend more and more on captive breeding in the future. With captive breeding comes an even greater responsibility, since we then have *total* control over their well being.

The moral obligation of man towards animals is well documented in the Bible. Proverbs 27:23 states "Be sure you know the condition of your flocks, give careful attention to your herds." Proverbs 12:10 states "A righteous man cares for the needs of his animal, but the kindest acts of the wicked are cruel." Therefore, I would like to ask that if you make the decision to enter into this business, that you fully accept the moral obligations and responsibilities that go along with animal ownership by providing humane and adequate care for your birds at all times.

Chapter 15

Decision Time
Not The Ending, But The Beginning

While this chapter represents the ending of the book, the preceding chapters have given you the information needed to start a new beginning in a business that can be enjoyable and extremely rewarding. You have seen that there is nothing scientific or complicated about raising parakeets, cockatiels, lovebirds or zebra finches. It is a simple, fascinating and rewarding way to either supplement your income or to make a full time living. The pet bird business is a well established business that is over 100 years old. It has not only survived, but it has thrived right through the great depression, too many recessions to list, as well as a number of major wars. It seems to thrive regardless of the condition of our economy. History has shown that people will spend on pets in good times as well as bad times.

I personally know people who have successfully entered the bird business and used the income to send their kids through college. I have known retired people who were able to enjoy a better lifestyle during their older years as a result of their birds. I have known handicapped individuals who were able to make a contribution to their lively hood as a result of the bird business. The bird business has helped many moms stay at home with their preschool kids. I knew these people well, I was their buyer.

I would not consider myself as an above average person in intelligence or ability, yet I was able to succeed and do extremely well in this business. Although I do not know you personally, I believe that if you possess enough intelligence to have read this book that you can accomplish the same things that I and others like me have done. While I have given you the information needed to succeed in breeding parakeets, cockatiels, lovebirds or zebra finches for profit, as well as the details on how to become a wholesale distributor of pet birds, the decision what to do next will have to be up to you. My advice to others has always been the same. Start small, make sure you enjoy the business, and then grow from there. This is a simple, yet little known business that has a huge potential. It can offer you a richer, fuller, more enjoyable life. This is America, the land of opportunity. You are the one who sets your limits. Aim high.

In conclusion, if you make the decision to get started in the pet bird business, I would urge the newcomer to be cautious when purchasing your initial birds that will become your foundation breed stock. Your success will probably be determined by how you start out. The information that is included in this book is based on years of experience and will shorten your learning curve if you will follow it. I have made recommendations in the book as to what to look for when purchasing your future breeders. Many times people will get in a hurry when they are entering this business and will want to buy birds that are ready to produce right **now**. It just doesn't work like that. This business is just like any other business. Some people will tell you any and everything, or whatever you want to hear, in order to make a buck. So be cautious. Please don't make the mistake of buying someone else's worn out breeders that they are trying to sell as proven breeders. Through the years I received many calls from discouraged people who said they had bought **proven breeders** from someone many months ago and the birds were still not laying. Most of the **proven breeders** for sale are proven not to be any good and that is why they are for sale. So be cautious when purchasing your breed stock.

I would encourage you to try to seek out reputable breeders in your area that you can trust, and purchase **young, quality** breed stock from them. As you read earlier in the book, we are retired from the business and no longer breed birds ourselves. In the event that you are unable to find quality breed stock in your area or people that you feel comfortable dealing with, there are several excellent breeders in Texas that I am able to work with in selecting quality birds for breeding purposes. These are the better breeders who have an excellent color selection. If you are interested in this service, feel free to email me at *info@petbirdincome.com* or give me a call at 830-895-5864.

We will soon have a new book available on how to build and equip a commercial aviary which will include different building designs and layouts suitable for both small and large producers. It will show in detail, step by step, including many photos on how to build your own breeding cages for the various species we have covered in this book as well as how to build your own nestboxes, carrying cages, feed troughs, etc. If you know how, you can build your own cages and other equipment for a fraction of the cost of buying them. For the people who cage breed their birds, building your own cages can save hundreds or even thousands of dollars, depending on your size. It will have many detailed photos that should prove helpful in the design of your operation. Our website *www.petbirdincome.com* will offer the book for sale as soon as it is published or you can contact us at the above numbers if you are interested and we can give you more information as to the expected publication date. Once again, I hope that if you elect to go into the bird business, that it will reward you greatly and enable you to accomplish whatever it is in life that you are striving towards.

Sincerely,

James McDonald

James McDonald

Appendix

Testimonials

"I can make more money with 100 pair of good parakeet breeders in a year than I can with 100 head of mother cows. By the time I figure my cost of the land, the cattle, the fencing, corrals, barns, tractors, trailers, hay baling equipment and veterinary bills, I cannot clear as much money per year with my cows as I can with my birds. Plus, I don't have to get out in the winter weather with my birds like I do with my cattle."

Dr. Lano Barron, (retired)
Agriculture Professor
Navarro College
Texas

* *

"My husband had 5 or 6 separate family members who had been raising birds in the Wichita Falls, Texas area for quite a few years, so we knew that it was a profitable business before we got into it. I was a beautician, but I liked the thought of raising birds because it would allow me to be at home with my two young boys. We started out with 100 pair of parakeets and through the years gradually built up to 600 pair. The bird business proved to be very profitable for us. Many years our income would range from $40,000 to $50,000 yearly. It turned out that I made much more money raising birds than I did as a beautician, plus I enjoyed the benefit of staying home with my young children. A few years back, the profits made in the bird business were used to build us a new house. After having raised birds now for 22 years, I can truthfully say that I have absolutely no regrets about being in the business, have thoroughly enjoyed it and would recommend it to anyone who enjoys animals

The greatest backyard business ever!

and is looking for a way to make income at home. The McDonalds were our buyers and we had a very positive business relationship with them through the years."

Joyce Van Huss
Beautician
Texas

* *

"My husband had became disabled and we were looking for something that I could do for additional income that would enable me to stay at home with him. We researched the bird business and decided that it was something that we could both do. We started with one building breeding parakeets, and because it proved to be profitable and we enjoyed the business, within a couple of years we expanded our operation with a second larger building and also began to breed finches. The McDonald's were very helpful in showing us how and what to do as we built our business, and we never regretted getting into the bird business."

Myrtle Clemmons
Texas

* *

"I entered into the bird business in 1977. We went to visit a friend who was raising parakeets, and before we left my husband told me that we were not going to buy even one bird. However, after our visit, even before we came home, we had arranged to buy 100 parakeets from them. We were looking for some type of business that we could start that would supplement our retirement when we reached retirement age and the bird business looked promising. We have never regretted getting into the bird business and have expanded several times. Although my husband and I provided the labor, the bird business paid for the materials that were used in building our new home. Now well into retirement, the bird business is still a very profitable business for me"

>June Vannoy
>Housewife
>Texas

* *

"I became interested in the pet bird business as a result of an uncle who was successfully breeding parakeets. For many years we sold our birds to McDonald Bird Farm, who in turn shipped them all over the nation. They were very helpful and instrumental to our success. Even though we only raised birds on a part time basis, the bird business provided the funding to send our daughter through Baylor University in Waco, Texas."

>Jimmy Box
>Vocational Agriculture teacher
>Texas.

* *

"Since 1983 gross sales from aviculture enterprises in Navarro County has grown from $100,000 to $350,000 annually. Over the years pet bird production has generated millions of dollars of income for the local economy and has helped to diversify agriculture in the county."

>Mike Gage
>County Extension Agent - Agriculture
>Texas Cooperative Extension - Navarro County

* *

The greatest backyard business ever!

"I worked in the data processing field and my husband was a news editor for the Associated Press. I was getting tired of the rat race and wanted something that I could do at home. My parents had raised parakeets for 30 years, so I was aware of the pet bird business. After I had been raising birds for a number of years, my husband retired and we expanded our business by building a second aviary. Our bird business has been profitable, as well as something that we have thoroughly enjoyed. I would not hesitate to recommend it to anyone wishing to have a profitable home based business. Including my parents, bird raising has been in our family for over 50 years."

Jenny Kellum
Data Processor
Texas

* *

"We were approaching retirement age and were looking for some type of home based business that we could get into in order to supplement our income. James McDonald had ran an ad in the newspaper stating that they were needing people to raise exotic birds to help meet the nationwide demand. We investigated the business and determined that it was for real. We started raising parakeets with one building and within 5 or 6 years had expanded our operation to include finches, and had built two additional buildings. Our bird business was not only profitable, but enjoyable as well. The McDonalds were very knowledgeable and helpful to us, and we would recommend the pet bird business to anyone looking to generate income from their home."

Ronald and Betty Tucker
Texas

* *

"We started in the bird business because we were needing something to do after we retired. We started out very small, raising parakeets, and expanded our breeding building twice. It was very profitable and provided additional income for our retirement years, but in addition to that, it was good for us because it gave us something to do. James and Brenda McDonald were very helpful in getting us started, and they were our buyers for the 12 to 15 years that we were in business. Because of age and health reasons, we are no longer in the business, but it is something that we would recommend for anyone wishing to make extra income."

Nathan and Era Rawlings
Retired
Texas

* *

"Many years back we became interested in the pet bird business because of our desire to earn extra income in a home based business. We have never regretted getting into the business. McDonald Bird Farm was very knowledgeable and helpful in getting us established in a profitable business that we enjoyed."

Douglas and Barbara Thompson
Mechanic and housewife
Texas

The greatest backyard business ever!

Veterinary Medicine Diagnostic Labs

ARIZONA

Arizona Veterinary Diagnostic Lab
2831 N. Freeway
Tucson, AZ 85705
Phone: 520-621-2356
Fax: 520-626-8696

CALIFORNIA

CA Animal Health & Food Safety Lab System
PO Box 1770
Davis Branch Laboratory
University of California, Davis
Davis, CA 95617
Phone: 530-752-8700
Fax: 530-752-5680

COLORADO

Veterinary Diagnostic Laboratory
Colorado State University
Fort Collins, CO 80523
Phone: 970-491-1281
Fax: 970-491-0320

CONNECTICUT

University of Connecticut
Department of Pathobiology
Box U-89,
61 N. Eagleville Road
Storrs, CT 06269-3089
Phone: 860-486-3736
Fax: 860-486-2794

FLORIDA

Animal Disease Laboratory
Florida Dept. of Agriculture
PO Box 420460
Kissimmee, FL 34742
Phone: 407-846-5200
Fax: 407-846-5204

GEORGIA

University of GA
PO Box 1389
Tifton, GA 31793
Phone: 912-386-3340
Fax: 912-386-7128

University of GA
Diagnostic Assistance Lab
College of Vet Medicine
Athens, GA 30602
Phone: 706-542-5568
Fax: 706-542-5977

ILLINOIS

Illinois Dept. of Agriculture
Animal Disease Laboratory
2100 South Lake Storey Road
PO Box 2100X
Galesburg, IL 61402-2100
Phone: 309-344-2451
Fax: 309-344-7358

Labs of Vet Diagnostic Medicine
College of Veterinary Medicine
2001 S. Lincoln Avenue
Urbana, IL 61802-6199
Phone: 217-333-1620
Fax: 217-244-2439

Illinois Dept. of Agriculture
Animal Disease Laboratory
9732 Shattuc Road
Centralia, IL 62801
Phone: 618-532-6701
Fax: 618-532-1195

INDIANA

Animal Disease Diagnostic Laboratory
1175 ADDL
School of Vet Medicine
Purdue University
West Lafayette, IN 47907
Phone: 765-494-7448
Fax: 765-494-9181

IOWA

ISU- College of Vet Medicine
Vet Diagnostic Lab
1600 16th Street
Ames, IA 50010
Phone: 515-294-1950
Fax: 515-294-3564

KANSAS

College of Vet Medicine
Kansas State University
Manhattan, KS 66506
Phone: 913-532-4605
Fax: 913-532-4039

KENTUCKY

Murray State University
Vet Diagnostic and Research Center
PO Box 2000
Hopkinsville, KY
Phone: 859-253-0571
Fax: 859-255-1624

LOUISIANA

Veterinary Medical Diagnostic Laboratory
PO Box 16570-A
Baton Rouge, LA 70803
Phone: 504-346-3193
Fax: 504-346-3390

MICHIGAN

Animal Health Diagnostic Lab- MSU
PO Box 30076
Lansing, MI 48909-7576
Phone: 517-353-0635
Fax: 517-353-5096

MINNESOTA

Veterinary Diagnostic Medicine
University of Minnesota
1333 Gortner Avenue
St. Paul, MN 55108
Phone: 612-625-8787
Fax: 612-624-8707

MISSISSIPPI

Mississippi Dept of Agriculture
Mississippi Vet Diagnostic Lab
PO Box 4389
Jackson, MS 39296
Phone: 601-354-6089
Fax: 601-354-6097

MISSOURI

Veterinary Medical Diagnostic Lab
University of Missouri
PO Box 6023
Columbia, MO 65205
Phone: 573-882-6811
Fax: 573-882-1411

MONTANA

State of MO Animal Health Div.
Box 997
Bozeman, MT 59771
Phone: 406-994-4885
Fax: 406-994-6344

NEBRASKA

Lincoln Diagnostic Laboratory
Fair Street, E. Campus Loop
University of Nebraska
Lincoln, NE 68583-0907
Phone: 402-472-1434
Fax: 402-472-3094

NEW YORK

NY State College of Vet Medicine
Vet Diagnostic Lab- Cornell University
Upper Tower Road
Ithaca, NY 14853
Phone: 607-253-3900
Fax: 607-253-3943

NORTH CAROLINA

NC Dept. of Agriculture, Rollins Animal Disease
Diagnostic Lab
PO Box 12223, Cameron Village Station
Raleigh, NC 27605
Phone: 919-733-3986
Fax: 919-733-0454

NORTH DAKOTA

North Dakota State University
Vet Diagnostic Lab, Van Es Hall
Fargo, ND 58105
Phone: 701-231-8307
Fax: 701-231-7514

OHIO

Division of Animal Health
Ohio Dept. of Agriculture
8995 E. Main Street
Reynoldsburg, OH 43068
Phone: 614- 728-6220
Fax: 614- 728-6310

OKLAHOMA

Animal Disease Diagnostic Laboratory
College of Vet Med., PO Box 7001
OK State University
Stillwater, OK 74074-7001
Phone: 405-744-6623
Fax: 405-744-8612

PENNSYLVANIA

Department of Agriculture
State Veterinary Laboratory
2305 N. Cameron Street
Harrisburg, PA 17110-944
Phone: 717-787-8808
Fax: 717-772-2870

SOUTH CAROLINA

Clemson University Veterinary Diagnostic Center
500 Clemson Rd.
Columbia, SC 29229
Phone: 803-788-2260
Fax: 803-699-8910

SOUTH DAKOTA

South Dakota State University
Animal Disease Diagnostic Lab
Box 2175- SDSU
Brookings, SD 57007
Phone: 605-688-5172
Fax: 605-688-6003

TENNESSEE

CE Kord Animal Disease Diagnostic Lab
PO Box 4627 Melrose Station
Nashville, TN 37204
Phone: 615-837-5125
Fax: 615-837-5250

TEXAS

Texas A&M University
Vet Med. Diagnostic Lab
PO Box 3200
Amarillo, TX 79106
Phone: 806-353-7478
Fax: 806-359-0636

TX Vet Med. Diagnostic Lab
Drawer 3040
College Station, TX 77841
Phone: 979-845-9000
Fax: 979-845-1794

WASHINGTON

Washington State University
Animal Disease Diagnostic Lab
PO Box 2037 C.S.
Pullman, WA 99165
Phone: 509-335-9696
Fax: 509-335-7424

WISCONSIN

Wisconsin Veterinary Diagnostic Laboratory
University of Wisconsin
6101 Mineral Point Road
Madison, WI 53705-4494
Phone: 608-262-5432
Fax: 608-262-5005

WYOMING

Wyoming State Veterinary Laboratory
1174 Snowy Range Road
Laramie, WY 82070
Phone: 307-742-6638
Fax: 307-742-2156

CANADA

Guelph Ontario Ministry of
Agriculture and Food
Veterinary Laboratory Services
Guelph Laboratories
Box 3612
Guelph, Ontario N1H 6R8
CANADA
Phone: 519-823-8800
Fax: 519-821-8072

Animal Health Centre
1767 Angus Campbell Rd.
Abbotsford, British Columbia
V3G 2M3
CANADA
Phone: 604-556-3003
Fax: 604-556-3010

Equipment and Supplies

Suppliers of cages, legbands, water systems, and other bird related products. This is an incomplete listing. There are many other suppliers, possibly some in your local area.

The following list of suppliers are listed for your convenience only. No endorsements are expressed or implied.

L & M Bird Leg Bands, Inc.
P. O. Box 2943
San Bernardino, CA 92406
Phone 909 882-4649
Fax 909-882-5231

Red Bird Products
P.O. Box 376
Mt. Aukum, CA 95656
530-620-7440

Wings Avian Products
9565 Pathway St.
Santee, CA 92071
Phone 800-447-CAGE
Fax 619-596-4008

Morton Jones
925 Third St.
P.O. Box 123
Ramona, CA 92065
Phone 800-443-5769
Fax 760-789-2740

Stromberg's Chicks &
    Gamebirds Unlimited
P.O. Box 400
Pine River, MN 56474
Phone 800-720-1134
 218-587-2222
Fax 218-587-4230

Bass Equipment Company
P.O. Box 352
Monett, MO 65708
Phone 800-798-0150
 800-369-7518
 417-235-7557
Fax 417-235-4312

Safeguard
P.O. Box 8
New Holland, PA 17557-0008
Phone 800 433 1819
Fax 717-355-2505

Valentine Equipment, Inc.
P.O. Box 639
Lemont, Ill. 60439-0639
Phone 800-438-7883
Fax 630-243-8882

The greatest backyard business ever!

Quick Order Form

Give as a gift to friends or relatives:
"The Complete Guide To Raising Pet Birds For Profit The Greatest Backyard Business Ever"

Telephone orders: Call 830-895-5864

Internet orders: www.petbirdincome.com

Postal orders: Brentwood House Publishing
P.O. Box 291992
Kerrville, Texas 78029

Name _____

Address _____

City _____ State _____ Zip _____

Phone _____ Email _____

Number of books _____ $39.95 each_____

Shipping $3.95 each_____

Texas residents add 8.25% sales tax each_____

My check or money order for $_____ is enclosed.

Credit card information:
Please charge my (circle one) Visa MasterCard
For the amount of $_____

Card Number_____
Expiration: Month_____Year_____

Name on card_____

Signature_____

Quick Order Form

Give as a gift to friends or relatives:
"The Complete Guide To Raising Pet Birds For Profit The Greatest Backyard Business Ever"

Telephone orders: Call 830-895-5864

Internet orders: www.petbirdincome.com

Postal orders: Brentwood House Publishing
P.O. Box 291992
Kerrville, Texas 78029

Name _____

Address _____

City _____ State _____ Zip _____

Phone _____ Email _____

Number of books _____ $39.95 each_____

Shipping $3.95 each_____

Texas residents add 8.25% sales tax each_____

My check or money order for $_____ is enclosed.

Credit card information:
Please charge my (circle one) Visa MasterCard
For the amount of $_____

Card Number_____
Expiration: Month_____Year_____

Name on card_____

Signature_____

Quick Order Form

Give as a gift to friends or relatives:
"The Complete Guide To Raising Pet Birds For Profit The Greatest Backyard Business Ever"

Telephone orders: Call 830-895-5864

Internet orders: www.petbirdincome.com

Postal orders: Brentwood House Publishing
P.O. Box 291992
Kerrville, Texas 78029

Name _____

Address _____

City _____ State _____ Zip _____

Phone _____ Email _____

Number of books _____ $39.95 each _____

Shipping $3.95 each _____

Texas residents add 8.25% sales tax each _____

My check or money order for $ _____ is enclosed.

Credit card information:
Please charge my (circle one) Visa MasterCard
For the amount of $ _____

Card Number _____
Expiration: Month _____ Year _____

Name on card _____

Signature _____